Praying
with the
Word

MARK COLLIER

Praying
with the
Word

W. Aubrey Alsobrook

PROVIDENCE HOUSE PUBLISHERS
Franklin, Tennessee

Printed in the United States of America

05   04   03   02   01   1   2   3   4   5

Library of Congress Catalog Card Number: 2001088957
ISBN: 1-57736-233-0

Cover illustration by Reba Terry Hunter
Cover design by Gary Bozeman and Elaine Kernea Wilson
Royalties beyond printing will be donated to the League of the Good Samaritan at Magnolia
Manor, Americus, Georgia.

PROVIDENCE HOUSE PUBLISHERS
238 Seaboard Lane Franklin, Tennessee 37067
800-321-5692
www.providencehouse.com

Where God guides, God provides.

In memory of Jacqueline, with gratitude for Alice

CONTENTS

FOREWORD

According to Psalm 1, people are "blessed" when their "delight is in the law of the Lord" and they "meditate on God's law day and night."

Being blessed is a good thing, of course, but what does it mean to delight in God's law and to meditate on it night and day? Notions of marathon Bible study sessions or all-night dormitory bull sessions on vexing religious questions come to mind. But when we look at the original Hebrew of the psalm, a different picture of the psalmist's intent emerges. What the psalmist actually says is that people are wise and blessed when they *"murmur* Torah night and day," and murmuring Torah refers to a way of reading the Holy Scriptures while speaking the words out loud, in other words a way of reading the Bible that blends study with prayer. Reading the Bible for facts and information is one thing; reading to draw closer to God is quite another. The first merely requires curiosity; the second demands an openness to the Spirit and a prayerful heart.

In this fine resource, W. Aubrey Alsobrook has provided a way of "murmuring Torah," of bringing together the study table and the prayer chamber. By joining Scripture readings and evocative prayers based on those readings, he enables us to let the Bible shape our prayer, and our prayer to guide our reading. He has helpfully arranged these readings and prayers around the great themes, such as creation, God's call, the Holy Spirit, and faith.

Aubrey Alsobrook gives us the prayer language to speak of our human condition before God. He reminds us that, like Adam and Eve, we have hidden from God's presence, hidden under the burden of guilt, hidden under an avalanche of activities, hidden even under moral goodness and the protective canopy of the church. He also gives us the free and joyful language of praise for God's rich gifts, words that ask for the grace that will enable us to make use of those gifts in the same spirit in which they were given.

This book, then, is indeed a way of "praying with the Word," or as the psalmist would have put it, of "murmuring Torah night and day." May it bring you much delight!

Thomas G. Long
Atlanta, Georgia

ACKNOWLEDGMENTS

I am grateful to Reverend Arthur Field, former supervising editor with John Knox Press, for his editorial suggestions.

I wish to express my appreciation to Andrew B. Miller, president and publisher, and the staff of Providence House Publishers for their professional expertise in the publishing process.

I am indebted to a host of persons in the churches and communities where I have served as pastor for their prayers.

INTRODUCTION

This book is an invitation for readers to participate in praying with the Bible. It is written for the general reader who is seeking a deeper meaning and experience of prayer and a greater awareness of God's presence through the Bible in his or her life. It can be used with family and group devotionals.

Praying with the Word makes us more available for the Word to become the lens through which we view life, as well as more attuned to hearing God's Word for us. In *Life Together*, Dietrich Bonhoeffer writes, "The most promising method of prayer is to allow oneself to be guided by the Word of the Scriptures. In this way, we shall not become victims of our own emptiness."[†]

In praying with the Word we hear God speaking afresh to us in the depths of our being.

In praying with the Word we join with the psalmist, "I have laid up thy Word in my heart, that I might not sin against thee" (Ps. 119:11), and with Mary, "Let it be to me according to your Word" (Luke 1:38).

Praying with the Word is using a brief passage of Scripture as the basis of forming our prayers and meditation. The more earnestly we pray God's Word, the more we will learn to treasure the Word in our hearts, and the greater will be the transforming power of the Word in our lives. We cannot encompass every human situation in one volume on praying with the Word, yet

---

[†]Dietrich Bonhoeffer, *Life Together* (San Francisco, Calif.: Hayer, 1954), 84.

wherever we drop anchor in the Word, God has a word for us.

Praying with the Word can pull together the fragmentation of our lives and center them more upon God. As Paul wrote in Colossians, "He [Christ] is before all things, and in him all things hold together" (Col. 1:17).

Praying with the Word can transfer us from the mundane to the heavenly and eternal, giving eternal meaning to life.

Praying with the Word exposes our sins, convicts, converts, and calls us to be disciples of Jesus Christ.

Praying with the Word brings healing, comfort, and hope.

Praying with the Word strengthens our faith, deepens our love, and enlarges our vision.

Praying with the Word leads us into the presence of God, for he speaks to us from his holy Word.

Praying with the Word transforms our lives and brings a new motivation to love God and our neighbors.

Praying with the Word enables us to know the will of God and deepens our resolution to do it.

Praying with the Word helps prepare us for what the day holds and what life unfolds.

Praying
with the
Word

CREATION

In the beginning God created the heavens
and the earth.
Genesis 1:1

"I am the Alpha and the Omega," says the Lord,
"who is, and who was, and who is to come,
the Almighty."
Revelation 1:8

Almighty God, our Creator, we stand amazed at the
wonders of your creation. We praise your name for the heavens
that declare your glory. The vastness of the universe reaches
beyond our imagination. The order and movement of the planets
amaze us.

We pray that the disorder of our lives will be ordered by your
Spirit.

Reorder our priorities by making you first in our lives.

Reorder our thinking from revolving around ourselves to
having the mind of Christ.

Reorder our wills to be submissive to your will.

Reorder our feelings of superiority to humility.

Reorder our time that we may wisely live each day in the light
of eternity.

Reorder our response to those in need from judgmentalism to
compassionate service.

Reorder the growth of our spiritual life to enter into the deeper
things of the Spirit. Create within us a clean heart and renew a
right spirit, and lead us in the way everlasting.

O Lord, we thank you for calling us into being, for sustaining us, for your promise to be with us to the end, and for enabling us to taste "the goodness of the Word of God and the powers of the age to come." In the name of Christ we pray. Amen.

Who among the gods is like you, O Lord?
Who is like you—
majestic in holiness,
awesome in glory, working wonders?
Exodus 15:11 (NRSV)

O Lord God, we bow in reverence before you. We are unworthy to call upon you. Too often our minds and hearts have turned away from you. Our obstinate wills have been bent upon doing what we wanted, rather than seeking to do your will.

Have mercy upon us, most gracious God. We pray for your forgiveness of all our sins. Cleanse our hearts, and set us free in your love.

It is awesome, O Lord, to stand before you. We seem so small in the light of your majesty and glory. Your power is beyond our wildest imagination. By your Word you have called the world into being, and by your hand we have been created. In your holiness we see what we are called to become, and to whom we are called to belong.

Our father God, you are always working wonders. We praise your name for the wonderful things you have done in our lives. Your Spirit has reached out and touched us when we least expected you. Help us to be more pliable in your hands, so that you may mold and fashion us according to your divine purpose.

We believe that you have many other wonders to work in our lives by your grace. We anticipate those wonders even now. As each new day dawns, we pray that we will be so conscious of your presence that we will hear even the faintest whisper of your voice. Amen.

You shall have no other gods before me.
Exodus 20:3

O Lord and Maker of all things, you have made us for you to be
God in our lives. Our hearts are not at peace until we find rest in
you. You have the first claim upon our lives by creation and by
making us in your image. You have called us into being and you
continue to call us to be yours. You have given your commandments
to guide us in your ways. Your love for the whole world has been
manifested in the highest by sending your Son Jesus Christ to
deliver us from sin and death.

In spite of all that you have done for us, Heavenly Father, "All we
like sheep have gone astray; we have turned every one to his own
way; and the Lord has laid on him the iniquity of us all" (Isa. 53:6).

Forgive us, O Lord, when we have put some false god or idol in
your place in our hearts. Forgive us, O God of Mercy, for forsaking
you, "the fountain of living water," for "broken cisterns that can
hold no water" (Jer. 2:13). Save us from just laying up treasures on
earth that perish, and grant us the wisdom and faith to treasure the
spiritual things that will last throughout eternity.

We pray for grace to love you with all our hearts, minds, souls,
and strength, and to love our neighbor as ourselves.

May you truly be God in our lives at all times and in all circumstances through Christ our Lord. Amen.

So I went down to the potter's house;
and there he was working at his wheel.
And the vessel he was making of clay was spoiled in the
potter's hand, and he reworked it into another vessel,
as it seemed good to the potter to do. . . .
like the clay in the potter's hand,
so are you in my hand, O house of Israel.
Jeremiah 18:2–3, 6

O Lord, how often our lives are like the clay in the potter's hand. They have cracked and crumbled. Our aims in life have not been realized. At times our dreams have been shattered. We have failed to be and do what you have called us to be and do. "O thou, whose deeds and dreams are one," we pray that our lives may be more completely in your hands. Mold and fashion us, Gracious God, according to your will. As we turn from one day to the next, touch our hearts with your tender hands and guide us aright. Remold us and make us fit vessels for your divine service.

O Master, cleanse us from our sins, and clothe us with your righteousness. Quicken our consciences to what is right in your sight. May the winds of your Spirit blow upon us and fill the sails of our souls, moving us through the day with the joy of your presence. Cast out our fears of the unknown, and fill our hearts with utter trust in your molding and directing of our lives. May we ever remember that this is best for us. Grant us true repentance, O Lord, for our pride. Grant us the assurance that our sins are forgiven and our transgressions are removed from us as far as the east is from the west and remembered no more against us. Amen.

2

PRAYER

When Daniel knew that the document had been signed,
he went to his house
where he had windows in his upper chamber
open toward Jerusalem;
and he got down upon his knees three times a day
and prayed and gave thanks before his God,
as he had done previously.
Daniel 6:10

And when they prayed
the place in which they were gathered together was shaken;
and they were all filled with the Holy Spirit and
spoke the Word of God with boldness.
Acts 4:31

O God, as our ancestors knelt and prayed and were filled with the Holy Spirit so that they spoke your Word with boldness, enable us to pray with such earnestness.

O Holy Spirit, so possess our lives that our prayers will be in harmony with the Father's will. May our prayers be more for others than for ourselves.

We pray that we may know that you are with us, as you were with Daniel, when we face our times of testing.

Transform our sorrows into blessings for us and others.

As we rise from our knees we pray that your Holy Spirit will go with us and use us in your service throughout the day: guide us in our responsibilities; direct us to some person in need; lead someone to us that we may encourage that person in their faith or give a helping hand; give us courage to share your Word and be faithful witnesses.

Then watch over us in sleep and prepare us for another day of service in the name of Jesus. Amen.

Continue steadfastly in prayer,
being watchful in it with thanksgiving.
Colossians 4:2

O Lord, we confess we need the power and witness of the Holy Spirit to lift the level and deepen the channels of our prayer life. Too often we have let outward pressures—things to be done, places to go, people to see, decisions to be made—consume the time and energy of prayer.

We pray for the Holy Spirit to teach and guide us in praying. So possess us, O Spirit of God, that our prayers will be prompted and permeated by the Spirit praying *in* and *through* us.

Grant us, O Holy Spirit:

A new listening to your Word in Scripture,

A new eagerness to the hearing of faith, eagerness to respond faithfully,

A new awareness of our situation—before the God of grace and glory,

A new awareness of "God's callings and courses in the world,"

A new awareness of God's redemptive work in us and the world about us,

A new awareness of our places and work with God among our family and friends, in our community, and in the world.

Gracious God, help us to truly pray in the Spirit, by the Spirit, and with the Spirit, and "take the dimness of our souls away" by the Spirit that the light of your love, peace, and joy may shine through. Wean our hearts from the things of earth, and make us attentive to what the Spirit is saying and prompting us to be and do. In the name of Christ our Lord. Amen.

Before he had finished praying,
Rebekah came out with her jar on her shoulder.
Genesis 24:15 (NIV)

O Lord, we thank you for answering the prayer of Abraham's servant even before he had finished praying. We rejoice in this reminder that you know our real need and what is best for us before we pray. We believe that in your love you only do that which is best for us.

Gracious God, grant that the lens of our prayers will magnify your will in all our thinking, willing, and doing.

We confess that "we do not know how to pray as we ought," but may the Holy Spirit so flow through our minds and hearts that our prayers will be prompted by your Spirit.

Our hearts are filled with gratitude for answered prayers of the past, for those that you are answering in the present, and for those that we will offer in the future with the assurance that you will be listening, O Lord, and will answer them according to your wisdom.

We lift our hearts in praise for the joy of your presence and for the gift of your peace in our souls. Direct us today, O Christ, in the paths in which you would have us serve you. As we touch the lives of others, use us to make their loads lighter and to help them know the Great Burden Bearer who makes all burdens light. We pray that we may be used to be the answer to another's prayers in the name of Christ our Lord. Amen.

Praying earnestly night and day that we may see your face,
and supply what is lacking in your faith.
1 Thessalonians 3:10

O Father of Heaven and Creator of earth, we thank you for all those who have prayed for us "exceedingly." We have felt the impact of the prayers of loved ones and friends. Our hearts overflow with gratitude for their prayers that were lifted to your throne of grace in our behalf. We know that their intercessions have been heard.

O Lord, we pray that our prayers of intercession will be prompted by and filled with your Holy Spirit that others may be blessed through them.

Gracious Father, we pray that what is lacking in our faith may be perfected by your grace.

Strengthen our faith where it is weak.

Enlighten our faith with greater understanding of your will.

Quicken our faith where it lacks zeal.

Enlarge our faith with greater visions of what you can do in our human situations.

Empower our faith to do greater works of love.

Establish our faith with an abiding steadfastness.

Extend our faith in strengthening the faith of others.

Increase abundantly the growth of our faith toward maturity.

Grant, O God, that we may keep the faith in life and in death and know the victory through our Lord Jesus Christ. Amen.

... the Spirit himself intercedes for us with sighs
too deep for words.
Romans 8:26

O Holy Spirit, we thank you for your prayers of intercession for us; truly your prayers go beyond our deepest understanding.

We confess we do not know how to pray as we ought, but grant that the Spirit will prompt our prayers, making intercession for us according to your will.

Open our minds to the truth of your Word.

Prepare our hearts to receive your Word.

Transform our wills to be obedient to your will.

Cleanse our desires and bring them in harmony with what you desire for us.

Direct our feet in the paths of your righteousness and service.

Clear our vision to see the needs of those about us.

Make us a channel of your grace to help meet those needs.

Take away the blinders of our pride and prejudice that keep us from seeing our own hearts as you see them.

O Christ, we lift our hearts in thanksgiving for your intercessions for us. Make our intercessions for others pathways of your grace for them.

Thank you, Lord, for the grace that has come to us through the intercessions of others in your name. Amen.

I do not pray that thou shouldst take them out of the
world, but that thou shouldst keep them from the evil one.
John 17:15

O merciful Father, we seek to lift our prayer of intercession on behalf of others as Jesus intercedes for us at your throne of your grace.

We pray for those who are tempted beyond their strength; enable them to rely upon the power of your Word and grace.

May your Word abide in their hearts so they will know victory over temptation.

Speak some clear direction to those who are confused and bewildered.

Awaken in those who are lethargic a sense of purpose in life.

Bind up the brokenhearted.

Comfort those whose hearts are bleeding with sorrow, and enable them to see your love at work bringing to pass good for them and for those who share their sorrow.

We pray for those who are experiencing unexpected turns in life. Lay your hands upon them, and grant the assurance of your presence.

We pray, O Lord, for those whose lives are in constant conflict and turmoil; help them to release their grip upon themselves and trust Christ in whom all things hold together.

We pray for your special blessings upon those who study your Word and seek to live out the Word in their daily lives.

Grant to us the mind of Christ and power of the Holy Spirit to keep us in the path of true life that leads to life eternal. Amen.

And he told them a parable, to the effect that they ought
always to pray and not lose heart.

Luke 18:1

Our Father God, we are grateful that you are a prayer-hearing and a prayer-answering God, and in your grace you grant us far more than we ask or think.

We confess our sins of failing to pray as we ought. Too often we have rushed off into the busy activities of the day without first spending some time in prayer. We have failed to understand our abiding spiritual need to meet you in the morning if we are to know your presence throughout the day.

We pray that the channels of our prayer life will be deepened by your grace. We know that prayer is to the soul what breathing is to the body.

O Lord, forgive us when we have seen only the dark side of our human situation and lost heart. Grant that our lives will be so filled with your Holy Spirit that we will not lose heart even in the most difficult and trying situations.

In our weakness, may we know your strength.

In our ignorance, illumine our hearts with the truth of your Word.

In our despair, fill our hearts with hope in Christ.

In our illness, grant us the touch of your healing grace.

In our sorrow, wipe our tears with the hand of your comfort.

In our uncertainty, grant us the certainty of your guidance.

Grant, O Lord, that our personal encounters and daily experiences will be seen in the context of prayer. In the name of Christ. Amen.

And I tell you, Ask, and it will be given you; seek, and you will find; knock, and it will be opened to you.
Luke 11:9

Eternal God, who has called us out of darkness into your marvelous light, we thank you for these promises from your Son about our asking, seeking, and knocking. We believe that you can "do far more abundantly than all that we ask or think."

We pray that all of our asking will be prompted by your Spirit. So fill our hearts with your presence that what arises from them will be in harmony with your will. Purify our motives. Capture our imagination. Direct our thoughts in the paths of truth. By your grace, may we indeed seek first your kingdom and righteousness.

O Lord, we thank you for your first knocking on the door of our hearts. We know that you have knocked and called long before we answered. May our knocking not be for any selfish purpose, but for more of your love and grace. Translate, gracious Lord, our knocking into open doors to serve others in your name.

In all our asking, seeking, and knocking, we pray for your mercy and for the forgiveness of our sins.

Direct us each day to someone with whom to share our witness to what you have done in us, and to listen to that person's witness to your grace in their lives. Brighten the light of our lives for your glory in Christ Jesus. Amen.

3

GOD'S REVELATION

He made known his ways to Moses,
his acts to the children of Israel.
Psalm 103:7

Eternal God our father, we thank you for your revelations of yourself. You have made yourself known to the children of Israel and to the world most clearly in Jesus who said, "He that hath seen me hath seen the father." We thank you, O Lord, for the manifestation of your presence and power, not only in the events of the past, but also in the lives of those about us. Truly we see your hand at work in many ways from day to day.

Confirm and strengthen our faith. In our times of doubt, help us to remember your mighty deeds and miracles of the past and that you have not forsaken us.

Lift us above pettiness and self-pity. Grant that our contacts with others may, in some way, be a means of further revelation of your love to them and to us.

Empower us to think clearly, to sense the feelings of others, and to respond according to your will.

We pray for those in hospitals for surgery and other treatment and those who are ill at home. Guide and use those in the medical field to be instruments of your healing grace. Be thou the Great Physician to each one. Be near to the ones who join us now in prayer. Bless them this day in a special way.

Enable us by your grace, Blessed Lord, to be receptive to the revelations that come to us in unexpected persons, ways, and places.

As you revealed yourself through the most unlikely persons in the Bible, we pray that we will be responsive to your revelations now. Amen.

Thou dost show me the path of life;
in thy presence there is fullness of joy
in thy right hand are pleasures for evermore.
Psalm 16:11

Almighty and Everliving God, we bow in awe and reverence before the majesty and mystery of your presence. As you have said by the prophet Isaiah:

For my thoughts are not your thoughts,
Neither are your ways my ways, says the Lord,
for as the heavens are higher than the earth,
so are my ways higher than your ways
and my thought than your thoughts (Isa. 55:8–9).

We praise your name, O Lord our God, for the revelation of yourself through your mighty deeds in creation and down through the centuries. "You made known your ways to Moses, and your acts to the people of Israel" (Ps. 103:7). "When the fulness of time had come you sent forth your Son to redeem the world" (Gal. 4:4–5). We pray that our minds and hearts will be receptive to your continuing revelations of your love and redemption. In the name of Christ. Amen.

He [Jesus] . . . asked his disciples,
"Who do men say that the Son of man is?"
Simon Peter replied,
"You are the Christ, the Son of the living God."
And Jesus answered him, "Blessed are you, Simon Bar-Jona!
For flesh and blood has not revealed this to you,
but my Father who is in heaven."
Matthew 16:13, 15, 17

Lord of light and life, our hearts rejoice in your revelation to Peter that Jesus is the Christ, "the Son of the living God."

O Lord, through the centuries and across the world, your revelations have been coming in unexpected places and to unexpected persons:

In the temple to a prophet,
In the fields to shepherds,
By the sea to fishermen,
In a tax office to a tax collector,
On the Damascus road to Saul,
In a monk's cell to Luther,
In a lay prayer meeting to Wesley.

We thank you Lord for your revelations to these and a host of others. We pray that our minds and hearts will be more open to the revelations of your will and way for our lives in the name of Christ our Lord. Amen.

... You did not recognize the time of God's coming to you.
Luke 19:44 (NIV)

O Lord our God, we plead for your forgiveness when we have failed to recognize your coming to us.

You have come in the words of another person but we did not recognize that it was you speaking.

You have come in a time of crisis in another's life, trying to get us to give a helping hand. But we assumed that there was nothing we could do, but you tried to get your message across to us to give a helping hand.

You have come to us through your church, and we were too busy with our affairs to worship you in the fellowship of the church.

Too often we have been so busy with our agenda that we failed to recognize your agenda for our lives. Have mercy upon us, O Lord, forgive and redeem us by your grace.

Yet, Gracious Master, there were many times when we did recognize your coming. As we recall events of the past there were profound moments and experiences when we knew that you were there.

You were there in times of temptation, shielding us from evil.

You were there in times of worship, speaking to us your Word of grace as the gospel was proclaimed.

You were there in the hours of crucial decisions, guiding us by your Spirit.

You were there in the times of sorrow and loneliness, comforting and sustaining us.

Help us to trust you, O Lord, at all times in sickness and in health. Amen.

And he said, "Go forth, and stand upon the mount before
the Lord." And behold, the Lord passed by,
and a great and strong wind rent the mountains and
broke in pieces the rocks before the Lord,
but the Lord was not in the wind;
and after the wind an earthquake,
but the Lord was not in the earthquake;
and after the earthquake a fire,
but the Lord was not in the fire;
and after the fire a still small voice.
1 Kings 19:11–12

O Lord, we confess that sometimes we think that unless you speak to us in some catastrophic manner, you must not be speaking to us. We fail to hear you speaking in your "still small voice." We pray that our hearts will be attentive to your gentle call and knock. Grant that we will be so attuned to your will that we will not miss your Word to us. May our eyes of faith be open wide with expectancy for the manifestations of your Spirit and the revelation of your will.

Enable us, O Lord, to hear your Word coming to us through the words, faces, and needs of others. O Holy Spirit, direct our thoughts in the paths of your truth that you want us to follow. We thank you for your truth that sets us free. Make us steadfast in your abiding love. Make us faithful in our obedience to your divine will.

O God of Light, we pray that you would take away the dimness of our souls by the forgiveness of our sins. Give us a clear vision of what you want us to be and do in the hours of this day and night in Jesus' name. Amen.

My kinsmen have gone away; my friends have forsaken me.
Job 19:14 (NIV)

O Lord, there are those who feel like Job—forgotten by family and forsaken by friends. Help them to remember that they are not forgotten by you. Grant them the grace to see through the eyes of the prophet Jeremiah who wrote, "The steadfast love of the Lord never ceases, his mercies never come to an end; they are new every morning; great is your faithfulness" (Lam. 3:22–23).

O God of steadfast love, as we look out upon this day, we see your mercies that are as fresh as the morning dew. We lift our hearts in thanksgiving:

For eyes to see the light of day and stars at night,
For your watchful care over us night and day,
For the eyes of faith that look beyond the shadows,
For every person we come in contact with today,
For the food that sustains us,
For those who share in providing for our needs, many of whom we never see.

Forgive, O Lord, when we have turned inward upon ourselves, rather than turning outward toward you and the needs of others.

We pray for those who have neglected their loved ones in nursing homes or elsewhere. Awaken in them a fresh awareness of love and caring in the name of the Compassionate Christ. Amen.

4

GOD'S PRESENCE

Behold, a virgin shall conceive and bear a son,
and his name shall be called "Immanuel"
(which means, God with us).
Matthew 1:23

Eternal God, whom the heavens cannot contain, we rejoice in your coming in your Son to save the world from sin.

We praise your name for your being with us in Jesus Christ. We thank you for not leaving us alone in the world.

O Lord, we confess that many times we have lived as though we were sufficient to live life without you. We pray for your forgiveness when we have ignored you and gone it alone.

We sing praises, O Lord, for the nearness of your presence. At times we have felt your presence in such a wonderful way. We have felt engulfed by your Holy Spirit. You were nearer than hands or feet. Shine upon us gracious God, by the inward witness of your Holy Spirit.

Thank you, Lord, for coming to us in the night and watching over us while we sleep. It is wonderful to know that "the darkness and the light are both alike to you" (Ps.139:12).

May the winds of the Spirit blow upon us while we sleep, preparing us to live the new day in your will and way.

We pray for guidance through the responsibilities and opportunities of this day, in the name of Christ our Lord. Amen.

As I was with Moses, so I will be with you;
I will not fail you or forsake you.
Joshua 1:5

O God, our Father, we thank you for your promises to Moses and Joshua and your assurance that you would be with them and not fail or forsake them. We thank you that your promises to them are also promises to us. As you sent them out on your mission, so you send us in our time to do your will.

We pray for minds respective to the leadership of your Holy Spirit so that we may clearly understand what your will is for us in our complex world. As Moses and Joshua went out into the unknown, grant us the faith to trust you for our unknowns. Underscore in our lives: *where God guides, God provides.*

Gracious God, as we look back over the way we have traveled thus far in life, we thank you for the touch of your hand upon us, especially at crucial places and times where decisions set our course in the right direction. We thank you for the persons you provided at the time and their words of wisdom and encouragement. We thank you for the persons who have crossed our paths with the Word of God for us. We thank you for those in whom we have seen a deeper meaning of Christian discipleship. We thank you for those who have challenged us in our thinking, and who have helped us ponder the meaning of life in the light of the Cross.

O Lord, in your love and by your grace, grant that our lives will, in some way, bear witness to your steadfast love and abiding presence throughout the day. Use us as we touch the lives of others in the spirit of Christ. Amen.

> . . . I am with you
> as I was with Moses.
> Joshua 3:7 (NIV)

O Lord, as you were with Moses and Joshua, we believe that you will also be with us. We thank you for your abiding presence. Your presence gives meaning, purpose, and joy to life. We thank you for the Holy Spirit that bears witness with our spirits that we belong to you.

Forgive us, O Lord, when we have wandered away from you—when we have walked in our own ways—when we have thought that we could handle our situations in our own strength. In your mercy, O God, cast out our sin and restore unto us the joy of your salvation.

As Moses and Joshua faced their task in the strength of your presence, enable us to face our responsibilities with the power of your grace.

Grant also, O Christ, you who were "a man of sorrows and acquainted with grief," your comforting and uplifting presence in our sorrows. Help us to see your hand at work bringing to pass that which is pleasing in your sight and is for our good. "In your presence, O Lord, is fullness of joy, and at your right hand are pleasures forevermore" (Ps. 16:11).

Gracious Lord, we believe that you keep your promises. We pray for your grace that we may keep our covenant with you. Be with us throughout this day as we seek to do your will in the name of Jesus Christ. Amen.

The more I call them, the more they went from me;
they kept sacrificing to the Baals, and burning incense to idols.
Hosea 11:2

O Lord our God, how often you have called and we failed to answer. We were so focused on what we were doing that our minds were blank regarding what you might want of us. This has led us farther and farther away from you. We have even forgotten the first commandment.

Dear Lord, you know where we are in our relationship to you. We pray for your mercy and forgiveness of our sin of going away from you.

In the midst of this day, help us to draw nearer to you. Fulfill in our hearts, gracious God, the promise, "Draw near to God and he will draw near to you" (James 4:8). We confess that without your grace we could not move one step toward you.

We pray that you will draw us into a deeper relationship with you. Surround us with your steadfast love. Enfold us in your abiding presence. Uphold us with your divine power. Guide us by your Holy Spirit. Transform us into the persons you created us to be. Enlighten us with the truth of your Word. Empower us to do your will. Use us in some way today to show forth your love in the name of Jesus our Savior. Amen.

My soul longs, yea, faints for the courts of the Lord;
my heart and flesh sing for joy to the living God.
Even the sparrow finds a home, and the swallow a nest for
herself, where she may lay her young, at thy altars,
O Lord of hosts, my King and my God.
Psalm 84:2–3

Almighty and eternal God, we praise your name for your presence with us represented by the holy altar. Your houses of worship, O Lord, remind us of your presence and the work of your Holy Spirit in our midst.

Gracious God, why is it that even the sparrows and swallows "find a home near your altars," yet multitudes of humankind are pulled by the tides of the world away from the altars of your presence. Holy Father, your heart must be grieved by the wanderings and waywardness of your children.

Dear Master, guide and use us today in some way to help a wanderer to hear your call and to find the way to your altar to praise, worship, and serve you.

Our hearts are filled with gratitude for the wonderful blessings that come to us through your church. We thank you for those who reached out to us when we drifted and were uncertain about which path to take. We thank you for their prayers and their caring. We are grateful for those who have been encouragers to us along life's way with the light of their spirits, with their words of wisdom that have lifted us above despair, and with their deeds of love and laughter. We pray for grace to be an encourager to others in the spirit of Christ. Amen.

5

GOD'S CALL

Now the Lord said to Abram,
"Go from your country and your kindred and your father's
house to the land that I will show you. . . ."
so Abram went, as the Lord had told him.
Genesis 12:1–2, 4

O Lord of life, who called Abram to leave his familiar home and go to an unknown land that you would show him, we thank you for his obedience. Abram, the "Knight of Faith," holds before us what it means to believe. He sets the noblest example of faith for all.

As we live this day, we pray that we may be sensitive to your call and act with unquestioned obedience. Let not despair drain our strength, nor fear chill our faith.

Gracious Father, cast out our fears of the unknown, and fill our hearts with a childlike trust in you. Cast out our anxieties about what tomorrow may bring, and open our eyes to see the opportunities to serve you today.

Fulfill your promise in us, O Lord, that "those who wait for the Lord shall renew their strength." Forgive our impatience and our unwillingness to be still and wait in your presence for your Word and the strength that you alone can supply. We do not pray to get rid of dangers, risks, and burdens, but to be given your strength. When we are overconfident, help us to see our weakness. In our weakness, make us strong in your grace. In our strength, help us to see our weakness.

Holy Father, when we pull up anchor from this world, grant us the assurance of your abiding presence as we depart this life and enter the world to come. Be thou our Good Shepherd then as you have been in our journey of faith. In the name of our Savior we pray. Amen.

God called to him from within the bush,
"Moses! Moses!" and Moses said,
"Here I am."
Exodus 3:4–5 (NIV)

O Lord, we believe that as you called Moses by name from the burning bush, so you call us by name. As Moses heard your call on the side of Mount Horeb, we pray that our minds and hearts will be attentive to your call wherever we are and in whatever circumstances surround us.

Gracious God, we know that you are more eager to listen to the prayers and cries of our hearts than we are to pray. As you saw the sufferings of your people in bondage in Egypt, heard their cries, and knew their anguish of spirit, so look compassionately on us and guide us through our troubled waters by your Spirit.

As Moses answered your call, "Here I am," grant us the grace and eagerness to put our lives at your command with our affirmation, "Here I am!" Prepare us to answer whatever your call is and wherever or to whomever you send us.

We pray that we may not be deceived by the enchantment of some distant place to serve you or of some great act, and fail to do your will in that which is at hand.

Forgive us, O Lord, when we have made excuses for not answering your call to tasks beyond our strength and forgetting your promise, "I will be with you." May the light of your countenance fall upon us to assure us that you are "an ever-present help" through Jesus Christ our Lord. Amen.

> My people are bent on turning away from me . . .
> how can I give you up, O Ephraim!
> How can I hand you over, O Israel!
> Hosea 11:7–8

Almighty and everlasting God, we confess that we too are bent to turn away from you, or to turn a deaf ear toward you, and to go it alone. We have so much to do, and the pressures of life keep us from including you in our agenda. Lord, especially when things seem to be going well, in our pride we think that we are sufficient. However in our heart of hearts we know that we are not adequate for life and especially for death. In our prosperity and in our want, we always stand in the need of your grace.

O gracious God, we thank you for not giving up on any of us. You are the Good Shepherd who goes out in our cities, towns, villages, neighborhoods, and to the ends of the earth with a heart of compassion for the lost. Lord, we know that it is not your will that any should be lost, but that all come into a knowledge of your redemption from sin and of the life that is eternal in Christ Jesus. We give thanks . . .

You continue to reach out to us in your steadfast love that never ceases.

You are always seeking us out, even in the faraway places of the earth.

Your mercies never come to an end, "they are new every morning."

You will never hand us over to Satan and the powers of evil. O God, we pray that you will make us strong in your grace so that we will not hand our lives over to Satan.

Your faithfulness is great, O Lord; we pray for grace and the power of the Holy Spirit that will enable us to do your will from day to day. May our lives be so transformed by your Spirit that we will unquestionably be witnesses for our Lord. Amen.

Come, I will send you to Pharaoh
that you may bring forth my people,
the sons of Israel, out of Egypt.
Exodus 3:10

O Lord, the giver of life, in the stillness of the hour and quietness of the moment, help us to hear your call to come to you. Grant that we will lay aside those things that would block your voice from getting through to us. May we come as we are:
  With our sins of omission and commission,
  With our burdens and cares,
  With our frustrations,
  With the pressures upon our minds and hearts,
  With our human frailties,
  With our often imperfect interpersonal relationships,
  With our joys,
  With our hopes.
  As we come to you, O Lord, we know that you have something for us to be and do as you did for Moses. We thank you for the opportunities that come our way to serve today. By your providential hand, we have been brought to this day. Guide us by your Holy Spirit to the tasks and relationships where we can best serve you. Make us an instrument of your grace that we may be a blessing to your holy name. Amen.

Moses and Aaron did just as the Lord commanded them.
Moses was eighty years old and Aaron eighty-three
when they spoke to Pharaoh.
Exodus 7:6–7 (NIV)

O Lord, you are faithful in all your promises, and we are grateful when your children are obedient to your commands. We pray for your forgiveness when we have failed to do your will.

Forgive our failure to listen to your call.

Forgive our stubbornness in not yielding our wills to your will.

Forgive our self-centeredness in thinking that we are sufficient.

Forgive our lack of faith in not trusting you completely.

Forgive our nearsightedness and limited vision of your Kingdom.

Forgive our narrowmindedness, and help us to enlarge our world view.

Forgive our coldness of heart and lack of compassion for the sufferings of others.

Forgive us when we have made excuses not to serve you because of our age.

Grant us the grace, gracious Father, to realize that regardless of our age, we can serve you as Moses and Aaron did in their eighties.

Create within us clean hearts, O God, and renew right spirits within us that we may more perfectly magnify your name through Jesus Christ our Savior. Amen.

> After the death of Moses the servant of the Lord,
> the Lord said to Joshua . . . As I was with Moses, so I will
> be with you. . . . Be strong and courageous, because
> you will lead these people to inhabit the land
> I swore to their forefathers to give them.
> Joshua 1:1, 5–6 (NIV)

O Lord our God, you have a way of calling persons to tasks and missions beyond their powers as you called and sent Moses and Joshua. We thank you for your call to us to walk in your ways. Grant us attentive minds and committed spirits to follow you with a steadfast faith.

May we say as did Isaiah of old spoke, "Here I am, send me."

We pray for the strength and courage to follow in the way you lead. Cast out any fears that would deflect us from your directions and purpose for our lives.

As Moses was your servant, O Lord, we pray that we too may be your servants:

Cast out our pride that binds us to ourselves and alienates us from you.

Enlarge our vision and understanding of what it means to be your servant.

Deepen the channels of our hearts that we may love you with our whole beings.

Grant us the faith and courage to face an unknown future, knowing that when our lives are in your hands we can fulfill your mission in the name of Jesus Christ our Lord. Amen.

The Lord came and stood there,
calling as at the other times,
"Samuel! Samuel!"
Then Samuel said, "Speak,
for your servant is listening."
1 Samuel: 3:10 (NIV)

O Lord, our Lord, we thank you for being the *calling* God! As you called Samuel by name, so you have called us. However, many times we have not heard your call because we did not expect you to call us, and so we were not listening.

Merciful Lord, we pray for your forgiveness for our sin of not caring enough to listen for your call. Forgive us for thinking that doing something else was more important. Forgive us for not expecting your call to come in our common experiences of life. Forgive us for thinking that you had to speak in some spectacular manner.

Quiet our minds. Still the thoughts of our hearts, and grant that our ears will be attentive to your call, O Lord, in whatever form you speak.

Gracious God, we pray that we will truly be one in spirit with Samuel as he said, "I'm listening, what do you want me to do?" Grant us the grace to be attentive to your call and to be obedient and faithful in the task to which you call us. Make us mindful that being what you want us to be and laboring in your name are not in vain.

Holy Father, we pray that in our listening and doing, we will be the persons you have called us to be by your grace revealed in Christ our Lord. Amen.

6

GOD'S MIGHTY DEEDS

For the Mighty One has done great things for me—
holy is his name.
Luke 1:49 (NIV)

O Holy and Mighty God, you have done great things for me:
You have called me into being—breathing into me the breath of life.

You have been with me amid the changing circumstances of life.

You have surrounded me with good influences by those you have touched.

You have provided for my needs.

You have given your prevenient grace that has come before me.

You have given your Son to atone for my sins on the Cross and raised him for my justification.

You have been my Good Shepherd to lead and guide me.

You have given ultimate meaning and purpose for my life.

You have given your Holy Spirit to bear witness with my spirit that I am yours and belong to you.

You have blessed and used the talents you have given me.

You have filled my heart with joy and peace.

You have opened one door after another to allow me to serve you.

You have given your healing grace abundantly.

You have given sight in the face of impending blindness.

O Mighty One, your doing for me never ceases. Grant that my love and gratitude likewise will never cease in the name of Jesus Christ. Amen.

GOD'S MIGHTY DEEDS

He provided redemption for his people; he ordained his
covenant forever—holy and awesome is his name.
Psalm 111:9 (NIV)

O Lord, our God and Savior, our hearts are filled with overflowing gratitude for the wonderful and great things you have done for us.

You have given us the precious gift of life.

You have sustained us all the days of our lives and brought us to this new day—a day in which no one has ever lived before.

You have provided redemption for our souls through faith in Jesus Christ, your Son, our Savior.

You have given us the gift of faith to believe in and trust your amazing grace.

You have opened the windows of heaven and showered upon us blessings of your Holy Spirit that are more than can be numbered.

You have opened our understanding of your Word as we have read and pondered the Scriptures.

You have kept your covenant with your people and with the world of humankind.

You have watched over us during the night of sleep.

O Lord, we lift our hearts in praise and thanksgiving for all your mighty deeds in the world and in our hearts through Christ. Amen.

7

GOD'S PROVIDENTIAL CARE

The Lord is gracious and merciful, slow to anger and
abounding in steadfast love.
Psalm 145:8

As a father pities his children,
so the Lord pities those who fear him.
Psalm 103:13

Almighty and Eternal God our Father, in praise and adoration
we turn to you. We come with grateful hearts for your blessings and
providential care. We have received from your gracious hand more
good things than we can number. Help us not to take life for granted,
but to recognize that every breath and blessing comes from you.

Open our eyes, hearts, and hands to the needs of others. Help us
to give ourselves and really meet others at their place of need. Enable
us to listen with our full attention when another is speaking and to
understand not only what they say, but also what they feel.

We pray for those who are ill in hospitals, nursing homes, and at
home. Guide and sustain those who minister to them; may their
actions be seasoned with loving care. We pray for those who are
near death. Grant to them the assurance of thy grace and peace. Be
thou the Good Shepherd to them as they go through the valley of
the shadow of death. May they know the life that is eternal through
faith in Jesus Christ.

Bless the ones who join us now in prayer. Be especially near to
them with the wonders of your love and grace in Jesus' name. Amen.

Seek good, not evil, that you may live.
Then the Lord God Almighty will be with you . . .
Amos 5:14 (NIV)

God of the Ages, by whose hand we are fed, we praise your name for all your blessings. We thank you for this day and the opportunities that come with it to serve you.

God of Light, open our eyes to see the good in the persons we meet today. Help us also to take time to see something of the beauty of the world around us. We confess that often we have not been still to behold the wonders of your creation. We pray that in such ways our lives will be focused on the good and not the evil.

Gracious God, we thank you for your abiding presence in our lives. Truly to be in your presence is life at its highest and best. We confess we have not loved you with our whole hearts. Have mercy upon us, O Lord, and forgive us.

Use us in some way today to touch the lives of others for good. May the light of your countenance shine upon us that we may think the good, sense the good, speak the good, and do the good.

Lord God, grant us the grace to give in the same spirit in which you have so graciously given to us.

Fulfill in our lives your promise, "Resist the devil and he will flee from you. Draw near to God and he will draw near to you" (James 4:7–8). We pray for the power of your grace in us to resist the devil and to draw near you. We offer our prayer in Jesus' name. Amen.

Then God said, "Let the land produce vegetation:
seed-bearing plants and trees on the land that bear fruit
with seed in it, according to their various kinds."
And it was so.
Genesis 1:11 (NIV)

O Lord, when we cut open an apple and see the abundance of seed, we are reminded of your great generosity. You have provided enough seed in the apples on one tree to produce an apple orchard.

Dear Lord, regardless of which way we turn in our lives, we see the wonders of your love and care for us. We lift our hearts in gratitude for your generous provisions for us and blessings upon us.

Guide us as we share what you have done for us and in us, that your gifts may be a blessing in the lives of others.

Through the miracles of your grace, Lord Jesus, use our words and deeds of compassion and caring to send a chain reaction of your love that will know no end as it touches the lives of others.

We pray that our lives will be fruitful in the things of the Spirit. So fill our hearts with the Holy Spirit that we will give a faithful witness for you in even the most difficult situations.

Almighty God, we pray that our faith will be increased; quicken our zeal that we may bear the fruit you intended for us to bear through Christ our Lord. Amen.

Even to your old age and gray hairs
I am he, I am he who will sustain you.
I have made you and I will carry you;
I will sustain you and I will rescue you.
Isaiah 46:4 (NIV)

All powerful God, we praise you for sustaining us in our daily life.

You sustain us in our childhood and youth with love and caring in families and by friends.

You sustain us in our going out and coming in.

You sustain us by your promises through all of life.

You sustain us in the bonds of your forgiving love through faith in Jesus Christ.

You sustain and guide us by the power of your Holy Spirit.

You sustain us in times of sorrow with the abiding presence of the Comforter.

You sustain us with hope when circumstances seem hopeless.

You sustain us in our sickness with the presence of the Great Physician to bring healing and wholeness.

You sustain us in the bonds of Christian faith and love in the fellowship of the church.

You sustain us by your Word that rings in our minds and hearts.

You sustain us in our old age as we taste the powers of the world to come.

Our Father God, we thank you for your sustaining grace that comes to us in such a multitude of ways. Continue thus to strengthen us that we may live life to its fullest through Christ our Lord. Amen.

And I have said, "Only you are my Lord!
Every good thing I have is a gift from you."
Psalm 16:2 (TEV)

O Lord, our Creator and Redeemer, we lift our hearts in praise
and unending thanksgiving for all your goodness to us.

You have called us into being and given us life.

You have provided for us with food, clothing, and shelter.

You have loved us with an everlasting love revealed in Jesus Christ.

You have had mercy on us in delivering us from sin by your
forgiving grace.

You have given to us the gift of peace in our souls that the world
cannot give.

You have given us faith to put our lives in your hands and at
your command.

You have given us the companionship of your Holy Spirit.

You have given us love that binds us together in families and as
friends in Christ.

You have given us open doors of opportunities to serve you in
unexpected places and in surprising ways.

You are the Giver of our material blessings.

Lord God, we pray for the grace that will enable us to make use
of your wonderful gifts in the same spirit in which you have given
them to us.

Grant that every gift that has come from your hands will be used
in the advancement of the gospel of Christ in his name. Amen.

8

GOD'S SHIELD

After this, the Word of the Lord came to Abram in a vision:
"Do not be afraid, Abram, I am your shield . . ."
Genesis 15:1 (NIV)

Eternal God our Father, we thank you for the call to Abram not to be afraid because of your promise to be his shield. We pray that you will cast out our fears and be our shield.

Shield us from being anxious about tomorrow, and grant us the assurance of your providential care.

Shield us from yielding to temptation, and make us strong in your grace.

Shield us from the sins of the flesh with purity of heart in your love.

Shield us from the sins of the spirit by the witness of your Holy Spirit.

Shield us from ignorance of the truth by deepening our zeal to search and know the truth.

Shield us from covetousness of position by opening our eyes to the opportunities to serve you where we now are.

Shield us from judging others; help us to see others through the lens of their best intentions.

Shield us from prejudice against those who are different, and give us an understanding of our common humanity made in your image.

O Lord, encircle us with your abiding presence and lead us in the paths of your righteousness and service through Jesus Christ our Lord. Amen.

Our soul waits for the Lord; he is our help and shield.
Yea, our heart is glad in him,
because we trust in his holy name.
Psalm 33:20–21

O Lord, in the stillness of this moment or in the noise that surrounds us, help us to wait in your presence. As you have preserved our going out and coming in, shield and help us now.

Shield us from speaking hastily.

Help us to control our words.

Shield us from cowardice.

Help us to be courageous as we face our trials and sufferings.

Shield us from dishonest doubt.

Help us to believe in you with our whole hearts.

Shield us from false choices.

Help us to choose life's courses in your wisdom.

Shield us from weakness.

Help us to be strong in the power of your Spirit.

Shield us from temptations beyond our strength.

Help us to have the strength of your Word and presence as we face every situation.

Gracious God, our hearts rejoice in your presence and the joy of our salvation. Forgive our sins and keep us in your love in the name and spirit of Christ. Amen.

9

GOD'S TESTING

Some time later God tested Abraham. He said to him,
"Abraham!" "Here I am," he replied.
Genesis 22:1 (NIV)

Eternal God our Father, as you called Abraham and he
answered, "Here I am," we pray for your grace that we may respond
to your call with obedience.

Soften our hearts, prick our consciences, quicken our minds,
and strengthen our wills to do your will. Take away the distractions
of things, and center our lives upon being empowered by your grace
to meet our testing and our tasks.

O Lord, make us alert and ready at all times to follow your
command.

As we come to the tasks and the tests of the day, may we face
them with the support of your Holy Spirit and meet them in the
light of your will. What is the task to which you are calling us in our
family and personal relationships? What is the task to which you are
calling us in the church and her mission? What is the task to which
you are calling us in the workplace? What is the task to which you
are calling us in the community? What is the task to which you are
calling us in the wider world? Reveal to us, O Lord, how we can best
serve you, and quicken our commitment to obedient service.

We join with Ignatius Loyola in his prayer, "Teach us, good Lord,
to serve Thee as Thou deservest: to give and not count the cost; to
fight and not heed the wounds; to toil and not to seek for rest; to
labor and not ask for any reward save that of knowing that we do
Thy will." Amen.

_____

10

GOD'S JUDGMENT AND PEACE

The Lord does not see as mortals see; they look on the
outward appearance, but the Lord looks on the heart.
1 Samuel 16:7 (NRSV)

Lord God, we are grateful that you see where human eyes
never see. We often make judgments of others only on appearances.
We do not know from whence they come. Their secret thoughts and
motives are hidden from us, but not from you. We do not see the
hopes and aspirations that challenge their minds and command
their energy. We do not know the pain of their hidden hearts, but
you do. Though we share the common bond of community, their
universe is different from ours, and ours from theirs. Yet we share
the common bond of our humanity.

O Lord, help us to remember before we judge another that it is
by that judgment that we will also be judged. Help us to see the log
in our own eyes before we seek to remove a splinter in another's eye.

We pray for the light of faith to see others in the light of your
grace and gifts. Search our hearts, O Lord, and see if there is any
wicked way within us, and by your mighty power, cast out our sins.
Grant us instead a spirit of humility and compassion that we may see
the good in others and wish the best for them.

Grant that we will never be a stumbling block for another
person, but a stepping stone forward for them in Christ. Amen.

Then I saw a great white throne and him who sits upon it.
. . . And I saw the dead, great and small, standing before
the throne, and books were opened. . . .
And the dead were judged by what was written in the
books, by what they had done.
Revelation 20:11–12

King of Kings and Lord of Lords, the author and finisher of
our faith, before we begin the activities and responsibilities of the
day, we want to begin the day with you.

Before we engage others in conversation, help us to listen to
what you have to say to us.

Before we perform a deed, we pray that you will touch our
hearts with some act of your Spirit.

Before we start out on the fast lane, help us to wait in the quietness of your presence—to be still and know that you are with us.

Before we hear the noise of the workplace and the world
around us, may we hear your still small voice speaking in the
depths of our hearts.

Before we jump to conclusions in judgment of others, O Lord,
enable us to keep silent, and help us to better understand where
they come from and who they really are.

Before we see the faults in another, make us aware of our own,
and help us to seek your grace to overcome them.

Before we stand in judgment of another, we pray that we will be
thoughtful and prayerful about what we write in our book of life
today—a book which will be opened as we stand before the One
who judges all. In the name of Christ, we offer our prayer. Amen.

On the evening of that day, the first day of the week,
the doors being shut where the disciples were,
for fear of the Jews, Jesus came and stood among them
and said to them, "Peace be with you."
John 20:19

Peace I leave with you; my peace I give to you;
not as the world gives do I give to you;
let not your hearts be troubled,
neither let them be afraid.
John 14:27

O God of peace and goodwill, we lift our hearts in praise for the gift of your peace, the peace that passes our understanding.

O Christ, we pray that as you calmed the fears of your disciples behind closed doors, you will cast out our fears and grant us the gift of your peace.

Watch over those who are afraid at night, and speak your Word of peace to them. Grant them the assurance of your providential care. Divert those who have intentions to harm others into the ways of peace.

Lord Jesus, as you spoke to the waves on the Sea of Galilee, "Peace! Be still," and the winds ceased, and there was a great calm, so may your Word of peace to be spoken to all hearts that are troubled and tossed about on the sea of life. May they look to you to calm their troubled waters.

Lord, we thank you that in your will is our peace. Grant us the grace to desire and then to do what is your will in our human situations.

In your peace, grant that we may be peacemakers in the Spirit of Christ, the Prince of Peace. Amen.

11

NATION

Righteousness exalts a nation,
but sin is a reproach to any people.
Proverbs 14:34

O Lord, thou who dost rule over the world that you have created and now sustain, we pray for righteousness to be exalted in every nation. Grant your wisdom to those in places of leadership and authority in government that they may lead in paths of integrity and peace. Enlarge the vision of those in government to see with keener perception the needs of the people for a life of hope and fulfillment. Grant that all citizens of our land will have the grace "to maintain our liberties in righteousness and peace."

Where people can move more freely from one country to another, we pray that the bonds of friendship and understanding will be strengthened and enriched. Where there are still barriers, may they be removed so that the world of humankind will become more truly one.

In our limited world of human relationships, we pray for the grace to make all of our interpersonal associations expressions of your divine love. Deepen the channels of our caring. Awaken us to new opportunities. Strengthen and encourage us to share in your creation to make a more humane social order.

O Lord, we confess that we are part of the problem of national strife and brokenness in the world. We pray for your mercy; forgive our sins of failing to fulfill our responsibilities to help make our nation a nation of justice and righteousness. May your holy angels lead each nation in paths of peace and goodwill. Gracious Lord, grant that "saving health" will spread among all nations and that brotherly love will prevail throughout our land and every land. We pray for wisdom and goodwill to diffuse fears, mistrust, and hate, and to draw the peoples of every nation together in truth, peace, and harmony in the name of the Prince of Peace. Amen.

12

CROSS OF CHRIST

The governor again said to them, "Which of the two do you
want me to release for you?" And they said, "Barabbas."
Pilate said to them, "Then what shall I do with Jesus who
is called Christ?" They all said, "Let him be crucified."
Matthew 27:21–22

Our Father God, we lift our hearts in humble gratitude for
the coming of Jesus Christ into the world to save us and the world
from sin. We thank you that Jesus steadfastly set his face to go to
Jerusalem—that because of his obedience to your will, there was no
turning back from the Cross by him.

We pray for grace, O Lord, so that if we have not already done
so, we may be as resolute in coming to Christ as he was in going to
the Cross for our salvation. We pray that we will not crucify Christ
afresh by rejecting his hand of mercy and forgiveness. Grant us
grace to overcome our pride and make our hearts eager to accept
what Christ has done for us at Calvary. May we not try to prove our
righteousness, but be clothed in his righteousness.

Thank you, Lord, that it is by the brokenness of Christ that the
brokenness of our own lives is healed. He is indeed the "Wounded
Healer," who binds up our wounds and makes us truly whole.

Grant your mercy upon those who suffer in mind, body, and
spirit. Some are burdened with anxiety; some are lonely and feel
that no one really cares for them. Surround them and us with your
presence. Open our eyes to the needs of those about us. Use us in
some way today to reach out to another in the spirit of the
Crucified. Amen.

For Jews demand signs and Greeks seek wisdom,
but we preach Christ crucified . . .
1 Corinthians 1:22–23

Our Father God, we confess that like the Jews, we too have demanded a sign from you to give us assurance. Like the Greeks, we too have sought wisdom to find you. Yet long before all our demanding of signs or seeking of wisdom, you were reaching out to us with your grace that comes before us.

We thank you that Saint Paul and others through the centuries have preached Christ crucified. Help us, O Lord, to let go of our pride and self-seeking and to kneel at the Cross with a heart of faith:

A faith to confess and repent of our sins,

A faith to believe your promise of forgiveness,

A faith to accept what you have done for us in Christ on the Cross,

A faith to live out your redemptive love in our daily walk,

A faith to trust our lives into your hands for time and eternity,

A faith to take Christ at his word . . . "Come to me, . . . and I will give you rest" (Matt. 11:28),

A faith to respond to the call of Christ in obedience,

A faith to put our lives at His disposal.

Dear Master, we pray for the grace to take up our crosses and follow you daily. Enable us by your divine power to bear our crosses in the same spirit in which you went to Calvary for us.

Grant, Lord Jesus, that by your grace our lives will be faithful witnesses to you, the Crucified. Amen.

13

CHRIST'S INVITATION

[Jesus said,] "Come to me, all who labor and are
heavy laden, and I will give you rest.
Take my yoke upon you and learn of me."
Matthew 11:28–29

Eternal God our Father, we thank you for the liberating power
of the yoke of Christ. We pray for grace:

To cast off the yoke of our selfish desires that lead us astray.

To cast off the yoke of our pride that keeps us from opening up
our lives to you.

To cast off the yoke of our fears that keep us from trusting in you.

To cast off the yoke of our clinging to material things.

O Lord, we confess that our lives have missed the mark of our
high calling in Christ Jesus. We have sinned against you in thought,
word, and deed. We pray for your pardoning grace and deliverance
from all our sins.

Help us to put on the yoke of Christ and learn of him:

To put on his yoke of obedience to do your will.

To put on his yoke of self-giving love.

To put on his yoke of utter trust in you, our Father.

To put on his yoke of servanthood—of one who came to serve
rather than to be served.

To put on his yoke of sharing another's burden to make it lighter.

O Lord, may we all—and all who also pray this prayer—bear the
"yoke that bears up the bearer" in Christ's name. Amen.

14

CHRIST KNOCKING
AT OUR DOOR

Behold, I stand at the door and knock;
if any one hears my voice and opens the door,
I will come to him and eat with him, and he with me.
Revelation 3:20

O Christ, we have heard your knock on the door of our hearts. We have heard your voice calling out to us. You have knocked and called in many different ways.

We have heard your call transmitted to us through the lives of your followers.

We have looked into some faces and seen the glow of your presence that called us to a life of faith in you.

We have heard your knock and call as some of your disciples have lifted their voices in songs of praise.

We have heard your voice, O Master, with a resounding clarity as we have listened to your servants so preach the Word and as we have responded, "That's for me."

We have heard your call, O Christ, in times of tragedy and sorrow, for you were there with your comforting presence and words of hope and assurance.

So, Lord, we have gradually learned that there are no times or places that are "off limits" to you; often unexpectedly you call us to open the door of our hearts and let you in to abide with us.

Enable us, Lord Jesus, to open our lives up to you fully, for you to live and reign within as our King and Savior. Amen.

For a wide door for effective work has opened to me,
and there are many adversaries.
1 Corinthians 16:9

Gracious Lord, as you opened doors for Paul for effective ministry, we believe you are also opening doors for us to do effective work in your name. We thank you for opening doors of Christian witness and service for us. Enable us by your grace to see and walk through these doors of service that swing open every day.

Dear Master, we, like Paul, face many adversaries that would keep us from entering the doors of ministry and service.

Deliver us from putting off to another day the opportunities that come today!

Deliver us from the excuse that someone else is more fitted for the task.

Deliver us from timidity of spirit, and grant us the faith and courage to act, leaving the results to you, O Lord.

Deliver us from thinking that we do not have the time for your work.

Some of these doors of service are near at hand, in our homes, down the hall, next door, down the street, across town, or over the fence, as well as in distant places. Blessed Redeemer, open our eyes to see the opening doors of service. Enable us by your grace to enter them with the power and joy of the Holy Spirit. Amen.

15

NEW LIFE IN CHRIST

Blessed be the God and Father of our Lord Jesus Christ!
By his great mercy, we have been born anew to a living
hope through the resurrection of Jesus Christ from the dead.
1 Peter 1:3

Eternal God, Father of our Lord Jesus Christ,

By your divine power, Jesus was raised from the dead.

By your great mercy, "we have been born anew to a living hope through the resurrection of Jesus from the dead" (1 Pet. 1–3).

By your gracious love, we enjoy life and the new life we know in Jesus Christ.

By your generous showers of grace upon our lives, our hearts are filled with gratitude.

May the sails of our spirits always be set to receive the winds of your Holy Spirit.

We confess we have not loved you with our whole hearts. Our minds have not always been centered on your truth. Our wills have not been submissive to your will. We pray for true confession and repentance for our sins. Cleanse our hearts by your forgiving grace, and set us free to do your will more perfectly.

Our Father, we pray for the church in all of its witness and service for Christ in the world. We thank you for its missionary outreach and pray for the abundance of your grace upon its children, youth, and adults, that many will be called and sent forth to preach the gospel and serve as missionaries in our land and every land in the name of Christ. Amen.

These are they who have come out of great tribulation;
they have washed their robes and made them white
in the blood of the Lamb.
Revelation 7:14 (NIV)

Loving God, as we reflect on our trials, we know that you have
been present. At the time, we may not have been aware of your
presence, but you were there: giving us strength for the moment,
holding out hope for the future when there seemed to be no future,
directing our thoughts and actions in difficult circumstances, and
opening doors where we thought there was no way.

Eternal God, forgive us when we have failed to put our whole
trust in you and when we have not believed that you were with us
in our difficult times. Forgive us when we have blamed others, or
even you, for our burdens and sorrows.

We pray that our hearts will be washed in the blood of the Lamb
who taketh away the sins of the world. Bring us at last to our
Father's house in peace, robed in the righteousness of Christ.

Empower us now, O Lord, in whatever testings and trials of
our faith we encounter that we may not be found wanting. We
pray for clear signals directing us in the right decision and way.
Open our ears to hear, our minds to understand, our hearts to
feel, and our wills to be set in steadfast obedience to follow our
Master's way. Amen.

While they were talking and discussing together,
Jesus himself drew near and went with them.
Luke 24:15

O Risen Christ, who drew near to the disciples on the
Emmaus road while they were discussing your crucifixion, we pray
for your nearness to us now. Our surroundings are different from the
disciples, but our need of your presence is as great as theirs.

O Risen Christ, as you walked with the disciples on the Emmaus
road and opened to them the Scriptures, walk with us today.
Illumine our minds and hearts that we may see clearly the truth of
the Word that is addressed to us. Save us from rushing past the
Word you are waiting to speak to us. We need your presence to
direct our thoughts, words, and actions.

O Risen Christ, who met with your disciples and bestowed your
Holy Spirit upon them, send your Spirit upon us. May the same
Spirit who inspired the writing of the Scriptures interpret them to
our understanding. Take away the dimness of our souls that we may
see something of the vision you have for our lives.

O Risen Christ, draw near to us as we face life with all its
demands. We need your presence in the midst of our daily routine,
as well as in our times of crisis and conflict.

We pray for your mercy, O Lord, and for the forgiveness of our
sins. We are human; we are frail; we are sinners; we cannot save
ourselves; we trust in your redeeming love revealed in Jesus Christ.
In his name we offer our prayer. Amen.

I know how to be abased,
and I know how to abound;
in any and all circumstances I have learned the secret
of facing plenty and hunger,
abundance and want.
I can do all things in him who strengthens me.
Philippians 4:12–13

O Lord and Master, we thank you for Paul's witness to your grace and sustaining power in his times of want as well as of plenty. In our times of deepest need, grant that we will look to you for the strength of your grace to see us through.

Help us, Gracious God, to see your hand at work in all the human circumstances of our lives and in the lives of those about us. May we not be overanxious about how things will work out, but instead trust that you are working to bring to pass that which is best.

Holy Father, from whom all blessings flow, enable us in our times of need to look to the abundance of your storehouse of love and sufficiency. In our times of abundance, grant that we will always remember the source of our blessings with thankful and generous hearts.

O Christ, you worked miracles of your grace in the life of Paul and enabled him to say that he could do all things in your strength. We pray that our hearts will be filled with your presence and power, enabling us to do all things in your Spirit and strength. Forgive us when we have relied only on our own strength, rather than reaching out for your hand to lift and lead. We pray in the name of Jesus. Amen.

He is before all things, and in him,
all things hold together.
Colossians 1:17

Almighty and ever blessed God, we confess that in our pride
and self-centeredness we have tried to manipulate and hold things
together by our own power. We pray for your mercy and forgiveness of our sins of seeking to go it on our own and live life apart
from you.

O Christ, help us to let go of the grip on ourselves and let you
grip our lives with the power of your grace.

Hold us together close to your great heart.

Hold us together in our faith.

Hold us together in your love.

Hold us together in our families.

Hold us together in our highest ideals.

Hold us together in life's ultimate meaning and purpose.

Hold us together and steadfast in our witness for you, O Master.

Hold us together in faithful service by your Spirit.

Hold us together in hope by your steadfast love.

Hold us together in our friendships.

Hold us together in our interpersonal relations.

Hold us together as a nation under God.

Eternal Christ, you who are before all things, the Alpha and the
Omega, and the One in whom all things cohere, we entrust our lives
into your care and keeping. Amen.

But to all who received him, who believe in his name,
he gave power to become children of God;
who were born, not of blood
nor of the will of the flesh
nor of the will of man, but of God.
John 1:12–13

O merciful Father, grant that our hearts will be open to
receive you in the fullness of your grace:
That our minds will be receptive to your Word,
That our wills will be submissive to your will,
That our hands will be open to the tasks to which you call us,
That our spirits will be in harmony with your Spirit.
O Lord, we pray for believing hearts:
That we may trust you with our lives completely,
That our faith will be that of a little child in utter trust of your
guiding hands and everlasting arms,
That our faith will grow stronger as time moves us forward,
That the certainty of our faith will become surer amid life's
storms.
O God, we thank you for the power that comes to us by
believing and opening our lives Godward. We confess that it is not
by our might, but by your Spirit that we become our true selves.
So transform our lives, Gracious Lord, that our thoughts, words,
and deeds will reflect the image of your self-giving love. In the name
of Christ we pray. Amen.

Therefore put away all filthiness and rank growth of
wickedness and receive with meekness
the implanted Word,
which is able to save your souls.
James 1:21

O God of Grace, take from us any wicked thought or motive.
Direct our minds in the channels of your truth, and enable us by
your grace to walk in the paths of your righteousness. Open our eyes
to see the beauty of the world about us. In particular, may we look
beyond our own imperfections and see the good in others. By your
Holy Spirit, destroy the roots of evil in our hearts that the fruits of
righteousness may spring forth.

O Lord, we pray for a spirit of meekness and humility that we
may receive the implanted Word by which our souls are saved.
Grant us eager minds to search and know the truth of your Word
that sets us free.

May your implanted Word permeate our whole beings, enabling
us to live our lives more fully for you.

O Lord, as we face every temptation, may your implanted Word
shape our thinking to make us victorious over evil as it did for Jesus
in his temptations.

O Thou the Living Word, Jesus Christ, so possess us that we will
always be at your command and be involved in your service. May
your implanted Word be the foundation of our daily living—making
us a blessing to others. Amen.

Including yourselves who are called to belong to Jesus Christ.
Romans 1:6

O Christ, you have called each of us out of darkness into your marvelous light.

You have called us from possessing ourselves to belonging to you.

You have called us from our self-confident pride to humbly trusting in your redeeming grace.

You have called us from turning in upon ourselves to reaching out to others in love and service.

You have called us from "being in charge" to letting you give direction and purpose to life.

You have called us from a sense of emptiness and meaninglessness to a life filled with abundant meaning and fulfillment.

You have called us from just thinking of the moment to seeing life through the lens of the eternal.

You have called us from our blindness to see the sufferings of the poor and homeless and to share in relieving their suffering.

You have called us, O Christ, from our fears of what may happen if we lift up anchor from a "secure" place to trust you.

You have called us from the ways of the world to your way of truth and righteousness.

Gracious Master, we pray that from the depth of our being we will truly answer your call to belong to you. Amen.

"And ought not this woman,
a daughter of Abraham whom Satan bound for eighteen years,
be loosed from this bond on the sabbath day?"
As he [Jesus] said this,
all his adversaries were put to shame;
and all the people rejoiced at all the glorious things
that were done by him.
Luke 13:16–17

O Master, as you set this woman free from her physical bondage of eighteen years, we pray that you will deliver us from our bondage of sin, and set us free to love you and our neighbors.

Deliver us from our self-centeredness, and set us free by your unmerited grace.

Deliver us from being possessed by material things, and set us free to love spiritual values.

Deliver us from pride that would vault us above caring about the needs of others, and instead lead us in humble service to others.

Deliver us from the errors of false reason, and set us free in the truth of your Word.

Deliver us from a defeatist attitude and spirit, and set us free in the optimism of the Good News.

Deliver us from despairing over human depravity, and enable us to see anew the glorious victory of the Crucified over the powers of sin and death.

Deliver us from a narrow view of what you can do in our troubled world, and enable us to see and believe what is possible by your divine power.

O Christ, we rejoice and give thanks for all the wonderful things you have done and will continue to do in our lives and in the world. Amen.

For since, in the wisdom of God, the world did not know
God through wisdom, God decided through the foolishness
of our proclamation, to save those who believe.

1 Corinthians 1:21 (NRSV)

Our Father God, forgive us when we have tried to know
you in our wisdom, to meet you on our terms, to make our will
your will, and to justify our ways before you, instead of listening to
and obeying your Word that has been proclaimed in Scripture and
in the preaching of the gospel. Deliver us, O Lord, from our pride
and self-seeking will. Have mercy on us, and forgive our sin.

We pray that you will place our feet firmly in the path of your
righteousness and service. Make us aware of the movement of your
Holy Spirit in our lives, and draw us ever nearer to the center of
your will.

O Divine Love, flood our souls with the light of your presence.
Strengthen us wherein we are weak. Awaken us where we slumber
in self-contentment. Lead us by your right hand to the tasks that
you have in mind for us. Transform our doubts into abiding faith.

Especially do we pray that you will use us as instruments of
your peace.

Enable us, by your grace, to always be at your bidding in the
name of Christ our Lord. Amen.

If you confess with your lips that Jesus is Lord and
believe in your heart that God raised him from the dead
you will be saved.
Romans 10:9

O God our Creator and Redeemer, surely, surely, you are in this
place with your love and caring. We confess that Jesus is Lord:
Because his love is shed abroad in our hearts.

Because he has taken away our sins by his forgiving grace.

Because he has given to us his peace, which the world can
neither give nor take away.

Because he has given to us the abiding presence of the Holy Spirit.

Because he has surrounded us with his divine providence.

Because his prevenient grace always comes before us.

Because he has given to us the abundant life filled with ultimate
meaning and purpose.

Because he has "delivered us from the dominion of darkness and
transferred us to the Kingdom" of Light (Col. 1:13).

Because he was raised from the dead and lives in our hearts.

Because our life is secure in his hands for time and eternity.

O Risen Christ, we praise your name for all that you have done
for us and all that you mean to us. Amen.

16

TRANSFORMED
BY GRACE

I appeal to you therefore, brethren, by the mercies of God,
to present your bodies as a living sacrifice, holy and
acceptable to God, which is your spiritual worship. Do not
be conformed to this world but be transformed by the
renewal of your minds, that you may prove what is the will
of God, what is good and acceptable and perfect.
Romans 12:1–2

Our Father God, we thank you for our bodies that are so wondrously created by you, and made to be the temple of your Holy Spirit. Help us to be good stewards of our bodies, and to so care for them that our health and strength can be used in your service. Grant that we shall present our bodies and our whole selves to be at your command.

We pray for those who are crippled in body and especially those who are confined to bed. Grant them grace to find in their circumstances opportunities to encourage with appreciation those who care for them. Be thou the Great Physician, working in and through those in the health professions to bring healing and wholeness.

Transform our hearts and lives by your divine power and reshape us within that we may more perfectly reflect the image of Christ.

O Lord, the world is so much with us, but we pray that we may be mindful of your presence in the midst of our home, travel, work, and other activities. Help us to see the events of the day as set within the framework of your providential love and care. Amen.

"O house of Israel, can I not do with you
as this potter has done? says the Lord.
Behold, like the clay in the potter's hand,
so are you in my hand, O house of Israel. . . ."
Jeremiah 18:6

O Lord, as the potter, when the clay cracked and crumbled in his hand, shaped it into another vessel, so lay your hand upon the brokenness of our lives, molding and shaping them to image you.

Gracious Father, we pray for your mercy and forgiveness for times when we have taken things into our own hands rather than waiting and seeking your will. Enable us by your grace to let go and let your hand be in control.

Control our thoughts by your Holy Spirit.

Control our wills by your wisdom.

Control our hearts by your compassion.

Control our ways by your guidance.

Control our imaginations by the beauty of your holiness.

Control our seeing by your vision.

Control our speaking by your voice.

Control our touching by the touch of your grace.

Control our going out and coming in by your presence.

Control our desires by the constraints and restraints of your love.

Grant, Holy Father, that our lives will truly be in your hands. We offer our prayer in the name of Jesus. Amen.

Seek the Lord your God,
and you will find him,
if you search after him with all your heart
and with all your soul.
Deuteronomy 4:29

O God our Creator, you have made us with a thirst that is unquenchable until we seek you with our whole hearts and know you in the depths of our being. We pray for your mercy and forgiveness for when we do not seek you first with all that is within us. We have let the pressures of time, the world, and our own egos possess us. Enable us, by your grace, to let go of those things within us, or about us, that hinder us from giving you the full reign in our lives.

Eternal God, our Father, we thank you that the first turning of our hearts Godward is prompted by your prevenient grace, the grace that comes before us. There would be no beginning of our search for you, without you first coming to us. It is always you who finds us and not we who find you.

Our hearts rejoice so that we sing for joy for the blessedness of being found by you. We pray that in the finding, we may go forth to serve you. We praise your name for wonders upon wonders of your grace in our hearts. Our hearts leap for joy for the wonders we see in the lives of those about us. Use all of us in the miracles of your love in Christ Jesus.

O Lord, enable us by grace to seek first your kingdom and righteousness, believing that all else that is needed will be added. Yet even as we thank you, Lord of Life, that it is not our finding you, but your first finding us that brings ultimate meaning and purpose in life. Amen.

And the Lord brought us out of Egypt with a mighty hand
and an outstretched arm, with great terror,
with signs and wonders.
Deuteronomy 26:8

Sovereign Lord, as you brought the Israelites out of bondage in Egypt "with a mighty hand and an outstretched arm," so have you brought us through difficult times. We thank you, Lord, for your everlasting arms of love and mercy that have supported us. In each trial, you have brought us through with signs and wonders of your unfailing grace.

Grant, gracious Lord, that we will not take for granted your hand that reaches out to us at all times. May our hearts be open and receptive to your will as you guide us today. Open our eyes to the needs of others. Make us sensitive to their hurts. Enable us to enter into their sufferings that we may help make their burdens lighter.

As we face our tomorrow and the uncertainties of the future, help us to remember the source of our strength and comfort. Grant us the grace to put our ultimate trust in you, O God, knowing that you will go ahead of us, preparing the way and preparing us for what lies ahead. Help us to not be anxious about tomorrow, but to live each day to the fullest for others as befits those who bear the name of Christ.

Merciful God, forgive us when we have tried to do our own steering, rather than seeking and trusting the guidance of your Holy Spirit in the name of Christ our Lord. Amen.

And he said,
"My presence will go with you,
and I will give you rest."
Exodus 33:14

O God, the Father of all humankind, we thank you for the assurance of your presence to Moses as you sent him on his mission to deliver your people from bondage. We thank you for Jesus' promise to be with his disciples as he gave them his Great Commission to "Go therefore and make disciples of all nations, baptizing them in the name of the Father and of the Son and of the Holy Spirit, teaching them to observe all that I have commanded you; and lo, I am with you always, to the close of the age" (Matt. 28:19).

Gracious God, our hearts are filled with joy and peace in your presence. When you are absent from us, we know that it is not you who have withdrawn from us, but it is we who have turned away from you. We pray that the winds of your Spirit will move upon us, drawing us ever nearer to you and driving the forces of evil further and further away.

Holy Father, our minds turn again and again to those mountaintop experiences in your presence when we were enfolded by your Spirit. In those moments, we too, like the disciples on the Mount of Transfiguration, wanted to remain there. We know that it is not for us to capture the Spirit, but it is the Spirit who comes to possess us.

O Lord, you have not left us alone. You are there before we arrive. Help us to trust your grace that goes before us and so is ever with us. Amen.

From his fullness we have all received,
grace upon grace.
John 1:16 (NRSV)

Lord of Life and Conqueror of death, our hearts overflow with
praise for grace upon grace that floods our lives, and:
    For your redeeming grace that saves us from sin,
    For your forgiving grace that removes our transgressions from us
as far as the East is from the West, so that you remember them no
more against us,
    For your justifying grace that makes us right with you, O Lord,
    For your sustaining grace that keep us steadfast in our trials,
    For your prevenient grace that is always coming before us,
    For your comforting grace that sanctifies our sorrows to our
good and the good of others,
    For your grace of the living water that springs up unto eternal
life within,
    For the grace and truth that came by Jesus Christ,
    For the "great grace" (Acts 4:33) that has been upon the church
in carrying out the Great Commission,
    For the grace of the inward witness of the Holy Spirit that we are
yours, O Lord,
    For your grace that gives peace,
    For your grace that gives hope in the midst of hopelessness,
    For the grace in Jesus Christ that makes us strong within,
    For the grace that humbles us,
    For the grace that enables us to grow in grace. Amen.

I give thanks to God always for you because of the grace
of God which was given you in Christ Jesus.
1 Corinthians 1:4

O Lord our God and Savior, our hearts overflow with gratitude
for your grace that comes with the dawn of each day.

The grace that washes and cleanses our hearts from sin.

The grace that set us free in the power of the Holy Spirit.

The grace that strengthens us for daily and sometimes difficult
tasks.

The grace that purifies our motives.

The grace that directs our minds in higher thought patterns.

The grace that clears our vision to see your will more clearly in
the needs of others.

The grace that quickens our conscience.

The grace that comforts us in our sorrow.

The grace that calms our spirits in the midst of storms.

The grace that enlightens our minds with the truth of your
Word.

The grace that focuses our wills to do your will.

The grace that prepares us for the events of the day before us.

The grace that moves our hearts with compassion for others.

Blessed Lord, we thank you for the grace that binds us
together in Christian love in the life and ministry of the church.
We pray for the anointing power of the grace of the Holy Spirit
upon the church for the salvation of the whole world in Jesus'
name. Amen.

Then one of the elders addressed me, saying,
"Who are these, clothed in white robes, and whence have
they come?" I said to him, "Sir, you know." And he said to
me, "These are they who have come out of the great tribulation; they have washed their robes and made them white
in the blood of the Lamb."
Revelation 7:13–14

Almighty God, the Alpha and the Omega, as we remember
that we shall finally stand before you in judgment, we pray that our
lives with opportunities, joys, sorrows, trials, and temptations, may
be washed in the blood of the Lamb and made pure by his
redeeming grace. We confess that we are not able to make them
clean—even our goodness is marred by hidden or open pride.

O risen and living Christ, we pray that you would take away our
cloak of self-righteousness and clothe us with your righteousness
received by faith. Grant us the grace to let go and let you have full
possession of ourselves. Help us to remember that the best preparation for life in the world to come, and also in this world, is to live
our lives in faith and obedience to your will and way.

Enable us, O Lord, to see you in the needs of those about us, and
then use us in your service in helping to meet those needs.

As the days come and go, may we grow in love for you and in
understanding of the mystery and meaning of life. May the communion and fellowship of the Holy Spirit be with us always, and so may
we be brought at last to the Father's house in peace. Amen.

For all who are led by the Spirit of God
are sons of God. . . .
it is the Spirit himself bearing witness with our spirit
that we are children of God,
and if children, then heirs,
heirs of God and fellow heirs with Christ. . . .
Romans 8:14, 16–17

Ever present God, we turn aside from what has occupied us to be with you in prayer. We pray that we may be led by your Spirit, having the inner witness of the Holy Spirit to assure us that each of us is your child.

O Lord, illumine our minds with your thoughts about us. Help us to see who we are in the light of who you are, Holy Father.

Search our hearts and help us not to be fearful of opening any inner door to you, but to know that your coming means light, cleansing, peace, and glory.

We bring our sins and pray for your forgiveness and cleansing.

We bring our homes to be blessed.

We bring our work to be sanctified.

We bring our hurts to be healed.

We bring our hopes to be renewed.

We bring our weaknesses to be transformed into strengths by your grace.

We bring our burdens that we may help bear another's burden and fulfill the law of Christ.

We bring our emptiness to be filled with the fullness of your presence. Gracious Lord, transform and reshape our lives according to your will. Amen.

Therefore if any one is in Christ, he is a new creation;
the old has passed away, behold, the new has come.
All this is from God who through Christ reconciled us to
himself and gave us the ministry of reconciliation.
2 Corinthians 5:17–18

O Lord, you who are the giver of life and lover of all persons, we lift our hearts in praise and thanksgiving for the gift of life and the gift of new life in Jesus Christ. We know that our lives are still far from what you would have them be. It is wonderful to know that you have not given up on us because of our sin and failure, but that your Spirit is striving each day with our spirits.

Forgive us Lord,

When we have not been still and waited in your presence,

When we have filled our lives with the things of earth, rather than with that which endures forever,

When we have not taken upon ourselves the burden of intercessory prayer for others as we should,

When we have been insensitive to the feelings and needs of others because we have been thinking only of ourselves.

Merciful God, grant us true repentance for our sins; cleanse us from all unrighteousness and set us free by the wonder of your forgiving grace.

Lord Jesus, help us to have an open mind and a teachable spirit regarding the Scriptures, that we may know the transforming power of your reconciling Word. Amen.

17

FREEDOM IN CHRIST

So if the Son makes you free, you will be free indeed.
John 8:36

Delivering God, we confess our need to be delivered and set free from the bondage of self-centeredness. We pray that you will deliver us from any false assurance that we are sufficient unto ourselves. Deliver us from a false sense of freedom.

We pray for grace to release ourselves from ourselves into the freedom of the Son, so that in freedom, we may know true bondage in Christ.

We thank you, O Christ, for the freedom we know when our lives are bound by your forgiving love, presence, and power.

For the freedom and bondage in knowing that our lives are in your hands.

For the freedom and bondage of your love that moves us with caring for others.

For the freedom and bondage of your Spirit that abides with us.

For the freedom and bondage of the witness of the Spirit that we belong to you.

For the freedom and bondage of your call to be your disciples.

For the freedom and bondage of your grace that keeps us steadfast.

Make us, O Christ, into instruments of your grace to be used in your service. Amen.

But about midnight Paul and Silas were praying and
singing hymns to God, and the prisoners were listening to
them, and suddenly there was a great earthquake,
so that the foundations of the prison were shaken;
and immediately all the doors were opened
and everyone's fetters were unfastened.
Acts 16:25–26

Almighty God, we praise your name for your mighty power
that sets us free from human bondage. We thank you for the mighty
power of prayer that links us with your grace that brings freedom.
Our hearts rejoice in the mighty power of the songs of the gospel
that set our hearts singing.

We pray for all who are bound as prisoners for whatever reason.
May they use their prison days to reflect on your Word and the
deeper meaning of life. Turn their minds away from blaming others
or blaming you, Lord, for their plight. Give them the grace and
wisdom to see themselves in the light of the highest that they can
know in your Word. We pray for the jail keepers and all who are
responsible for the inmates' imprisonment. May every avenue be
followed that leads to rehabilitation of the imprisoned. Grant
wisdom to the courts that justice may be done. We also pray for the
innocent who have suffered from criminal acts; may the way be
found for some appropriate recompense for their loss.

Break the bonds of sin that bind our hearts; open the doors of
our hearts to the mercy and grace of Jesus Christ.

In our shaken and shattered world, we pray for a resolute
commitment of our lives to Christ in whom all things cohere and
hold together. Amen.

18

CHRIST'S RETURN

And when he had said this, as they were looking on,
he was lifted up, and a cloud took him out of their sight.
And while they were gazing into heaven as he went,
behold, two men stood by them in white robes, and said,
"Men of Galilee, why do you stand looking into heaven?
This Jesus, who was taken up from you into heaven, will
come in the same way as you saw him go into heaven."
Acts 1:9–11

Heavenly Father, we thank you for the first coming of Jesus Christ as the Savior of the world. We thank you for his promise of his second coming. Help us not to be idlers, but to be faithful disciples engaged in Christian service. May we reveal our zeal for Christ by faithful obedience to him rather than speculation about when he will return.

Help us to treat each day as though it were our last. Grant that the lamp of our faith will be filled with the oil of grace and will burn brightly, ready for his return, whether early or late.

O Christ, we believe you will come to judge the living and the dead. We shall all stand before you to give an account of how we have lived. We pray for your mercy and the forgiveness of our sins.

Deliver us from believing the false prophets who claim that they know when you will return. Rather may we rely upon Jesus' promise: "Where two or three are gathered in my name, there am I in the midst of them" (Matt. 18:20).

Grant us the assurance that when our lives are in your hands, they are in safekeeping for time and eternity. Amen.

19

THE HOLY SPIRIT

And when they had prayed, the place in which they were
gathered together was shaken, and they were all filled with
the Holy Spirit and spoke the Word of God with boldness.
Acts 4:31

Almighty God, we thank you for the wind of the Holy Spirit
that has blown upon our hearts in times of prayer and shaken us to
the foundation. We thank you:

For the Spirit that has uprooted us from our old ways,

For the Spirit that has transformed our ways of thinking and
turned our lives Godward,

For the Spirit that has filled the sails of our souls and has driven
us into uncharted seas to find there the wonders of your grace,

For the Spirit that has burned with cleansing and purifying
grace in our hearts,

For the Spirit that has given us a new mind in Christ,

For the Spirit that makes us restless until we rest in you,

For the Spirit that sends us to our knees in repentance and in
faith in your mercy and forgiveness,

For the Spirit that strengthens our inner lives and empowers us
to witness about Jesus Christ with boldness and love,

For the Spirit that comforts us in our sorrows and leads us to
live in the light of the eternal day that is before us.

We offer our prayer in the name of the living Word, Jesus
Christ. Amen.

The Holy Spirit

The Spirit of the Lord is on me, because he has anointed
me to preach good news to the poor.
He has sent me to proclaim release to the captives and
recovering of sight to the blind. To set at liberty those who
are oppressed, to proclaim the acceptable year of the Lord.
. . . Today this Scripture has been fulfilled in your hearing.
Luke 4:18–21

O Spirit of the Lord, who anointed the Son to preach the good news to the poor, we confess our spiritual poverty and pray for your anointing. Help us to minister to those who lack food, clothing, and shelter. Make us instruments of your peace to set free those who are in bondage to alcohol and drugs. Use us to spread your truth to those in bondage to ignorance and fear. So light our lives that we may bear witness to your Light to those who are overcome by darkness. Bless our ministry to those who are in prison cells; may they know the higher bondage in Christ.

As we think of those who are oppressed by circumstances beyond their control, guide and use us in some way to relieve the suffering they are enduring. Help us, O Lord, to truly put our lives at your command to reach out to others in your name and Spirit.

Make our walk with you so close that there will never be any doubt about your walking with us. Flood our hearts with the anointing of your Spirit so that our lives will give an uncompromising witness to Christ.

Lord, make this a day in which the truth of the Scripture is fulfilled in our hearts in some way. Amen.

Take the helmet of salvation and the sword of the Spirit,
which is the Word of God.
Ephesians 6:17 (NIV)

O Lord our God, you alone are our defense against temptation
to do evil. We believe that as you delivered Israel from bondage in
Egypt, you can deliver us from sin by the power of your mercy and
forgiving love revealed in Jesus Christ.

We confess that we have not trusted you as we should. Too often
we have set out on our own. Gracious God, grant us your forgiveness and clothe us with your righteousness and salvation.

As we face today's temptations, burdens, joys, and responsibilities, may the sword of the Spirit, your Word, be our defense against
evil and our offense for good.

May we join with the psalmist when he said, "I have laid up thy
word in my heart, that I might not sin against thee" (Ps. 119:11). O
Christ, as you faced Satan's temptations with the Word of God and
stood steadfast while Satan fell, grant us the inner strength of your
grace to say "No" to the evil, and "Yes" to the good and true.

O Christ, you are the living Word; live in our hearts and
empower us to walk in your ways. Enable us to see and serve you by
the light and power of the Word of God. May the sword of the Spirit
cut away and cast into fire all in our hearts that is displeasing to you.
Almighty God, show us how to take the offensive against evil rather
than just trying to defend ourselves. Amen.

But the Spirit entered into me
and set me upon my feet. . . .
Ezekiel 3:24

Father God, we lift our hearts in praise for your Spirit's coming again and again to lift our spirits. Your Spirit has reached out to us when we faltered and set us on our feet. When we have been confused, wondering which way to turn, your Spirit has come to guide us aright.

When our hearts have been gripped by grief, your Spirit entered into us and shared our sorrow with its comforting presence.

When we have faced seemingly impossible tasks, the Spirit has strengthened us and enabled us to do the work to which we were called.

In the daily routine of life, O Lord, your Spirit has come to turn what would otherwise be drudgery into meaning and purpose.

When the outward pressures of life have beaten upon us, the Spirit has strengthened us. The inner witness of your Spirit with our spirits sets us upon our feet and sends us forth to live life in the wonder of your presence.

O Lord of Life, thank you for your Spirit that transforms our doubts into an expression of courage and faith. Your Spirit replaces our pessimism with optimism. Our sense of hopelessness gives way to hope in the Spirit. The Spirit quickens our awareness of the needs of others. The Spirit lifts us above self-pity. The Spirit casts out anger and brings in love.

For all the coming and abiding presence of the Spirit we thank you Lord. Amen.

> If we live by the Spirit,
> let us also walk by the Spirit.
> Galatians 5:25

Come, Holy Spirit, come!

Come into our minds and direct our thinking, reasoning, and imagining.

Come into our hearts and cleanse them of all sin by the power of your redeeming grace.

Come into the routine situations we face today and illumine them with your presence.

Come into our interpersonal relations, that they may reflect your love.

Come into our motives and make them pure.

Come into our dwelling and hallow it with your presence.

Come into our illness that it may be sanctified for our good and the good of others.

Come into our sorrow that we may see your hand at work, bringing to pass that which is good.

Come into our business relations that they may reflect honesty and integrity.

Come, O Spirit, into our daily walk that we may keep in step with you in your paths of righteousness and service.

Come and empower us to give a resounding "No!" to temptation, and a steadfast "Yes!" to the right through Christ our Lord. Amen.

And now, compelled by the Spirit,
I am going to Jerusalem, not knowing what will happen
to me there. I only know that in every city the Holy Spirit
warns me that prison and hardships are facing me.
However, I consider my life worth nothing to me,
if only I may finish the race and complete the task
the Lord Jesus has given me—the task of testifying
to the gospel of God's grace.
Acts 20:22–24 (NIV)

O God of Life, as your Spirit moved with compelling power in the life of St. Paul, we pray that you would so move in our hearts. He went to Jerusalem not knowing what would happen to him, but only that the Spirit warned him of hardship and imprisonment. O Lord, we thank you for St. Paul's commitment in such an hour to "finish the race and complete the task" of testifying to the gospel of your grace.

We pray that we may be steeled with such an ultimate commitment to live for Christ and bear witness to your grace. O Lord, we do not know what lies ahead of us, but we believe that you are well aware of what awaits us, for good or evil. May our preparation for the unknown always be with an assurance of your abiding and guiding Spirit. May we never turn back, but steadfastly lock our wills into obedience to your will. We make our prayer in the name and spirit of Christ. Amen.

When they [Paul and his companions]
had come opposite Mysia,
they attempted to go into Bithynia,
but the Spirit of Jesus did not allow them;
so pressing by Mysia, they went down to Troas.
And a vision appeared to Paul in the night:
A man of Macedonia was standing beseeching him
and saying, "Come over to Macedonia and help us."
And when he had seen the vision,
immediately we sought to go on into Macedonia,
concluding that God has called us
to preach the gospel to them.
Acts 16:7–10

Almighty God, our Guide and Redeemer, we confess that we do not always have the knowledge or wisdom to choose the way we should go. Sometimes we think that we know which way to go and what we should do, but it turns out that we were wrong.

O Lord, as you guided St. Paul from Troas to Macedonia, we pray that we will be sensitive to your Spirit's call to us. Unstop our ears that we may hear the cries of those about us in need. Open our eyes to see what lies before us. Make our hearts compassionate toward those who suffer in poverty and deprivation. Enable us to reach out as we can with a helping hand. Help us to "give legs to our prayers."

O God, forbid that we pass by on the other side of those about us in need. Stop us in our tracks! Grant us your grace to do for those in need as you would have us do. We offer our prayer in the name and spirit of Christ. Amen.

But you shall receive power when the Holy Spirit has come
upon you; and you shall be my witnesses in Jerusalem and
in all Judea and Samaria and to the end of the earth.
Acts 1:8

O Lord of Life and Power, we thank you for new life and for the
power of your Holy Spirit to enable us to live lives full of meaning,
purpose, and freedom in your grace.

We thank you for the first prompting of your Spirit to turn our
lives Godward.

We thank you for the coming of the Holy Spirit again and again
at life's turns.

We thank you for the guidance of the Holy Spirit as we face
decisions, decisions that sometimes are freighted with profound and
far-reaching meaning for us and others.

O Lord, our hearts are lifted in praise for the lifting power of the
Holy Spirit:

Lifting us out of a sense of hopelessness and despair,

Lifting our horizons so we can see beyond the shadows of imme-
diate circumstances,

Lifting us from our disappointments and sorrows into the joys of
new beginnings,

Lifting us from the clutches of temptation and sin into the joys
of your saving and abiding presence,

Lifting us out of our timidity and fears about what you can do in
and through our lives.

We pray for the presence of the Holy Spirit that will enable us
to be witnesses of Christ in the world about us. Amen.

These things I have spoken to you, while I am still with you.
But the Counselor, the Holy Spirit,
whom the Father will send in my name,
he will teach you all things,
and bring to your remembrance
all that I have said to you.
John 14:25–26

Our Father God, we thank you for the coming of Jesus Christ into the world to reveal the depth of your love and to redeem the world from sin.

We praise your name for the truths that Jesus taught, and pray that those truths will be woven in the fabric of our lives. We pray that the Holy Spirit will illumine our minds with clarity of understanding to grasp Jesus' teaching. Enable us by your grace to put into practice his teachings in our daily lives.

Save us, O Lord, from trying to justify our unworthy ways before you. Instead, help us to be open to the movements of the Holy Spirit to bring us into a right relationship with you and with others.

O Master, may the light of your teachings flood our minds and hearts and direct us in the way we should go. We pray that your teachings and the spirit of your teachings will permeate our whole beings so that our thoughts and actions will be in harmony with your will.

"Teach us, good Lord, to serve Thee as Thou deservest: To give and not count the cost. To fight and not heed the wounds. To toil and not to seek for rest; To labor and not ask for any reward save that of knowing that we do Thy will" (Prayer of Ignatius Loyola, founder of the Society of Jesus in 1534). Amen.

Thou dost guide me,
with thy counsel, and afterward
thou wilt receive me to glory.
Whom have I in heaven but thee?
And there is nothing upon earth
that I desire beside thee.
Psalm 73:24–25

O Lord, our hearts are filled with gratitude for your guiding Spirit and counsel. Time and time again we have come to you, praying for a clear sense of direction in varied situations. Your counsel has come in different ways. Sometimes by a thought and sometimes through another person, you have offered us guidance. Thank you, Lord, for being present with the touch of your hand upon our lives, as well as upon the lives of others.

Father, forgive when we have failed to obey your counsel. Mend our brokenness caused by our failure to hear and heed your Word and follow your guidance.

Grant, Gracious God, that we may be steadfast in faith, grounded in love, and prompted by your Holy Spirit to walk in the paths of your righteousness and service. We pray for the quality of faith that Abraham had as he followed your command and direction without question. May we have the assurance that our lives are also in your hands and that we can leave the *when* and the *where* also in your hands.

Merciful God, we pray for the grace by faith to be received in glory when we have finished our earthly journey in the name of our Blessed Redeemer. Amen.

Do not fear, for I am with you, do not be afraid,
for I am your God; I will strengthen you, I will help you,
I will uphold you. . . . For I, the Lord your God, hold your
right hand; it is I who say to you,
"Do not fear, I will help you."
Isaiah 41:10, 13 (NRSV)

Almighty God, our hearts overflow with gratitude for your abiding presence. Thank you Lord, for casting out our fears. In the wonder of your presence, fears are diminished and disappear.

Again and again, Lord you have come to us at the time of our greatest need. When we look back over our shoulders, we see that you were leading and guiding us. Thank you, Lord, for your hand that reaches out to keep us from yielding to temptation and that holds us in the path of your righteousness and service. Awaken in us a greater dependence upon your strength and guidance.

Holy Father, we thank you for your promise that you will help and uphold us. We know that your promises are true and are kept. We pray for grace that will enable us to rely on your help, to seek your guidance first, to listen for the Holy Spirit giving direction, to wait and be still in your presence that we may discern your will, and to reach out with a penitent heart for forgiveness of our sins. Grant that the love of Christ will permeate all our relations.

Lord, we do not ask to understand all the mysteries of life. We do pray for the grace and wisdom to live with these mysteries, to know the joy and peace of your presence even amidst them, and to gratefully await the glory that is to come in the fullness of your Kingdom. Amen.

20

FAITH

Trust in the Lord with all your heart and lean not on your
own understanding; in all your ways acknowledge him, and
he will make your paths straight.
Proverbs 3:5-6 (NIV)

Promise-keeping God, we thank you that your promises
are always kept. We confess that we have often relied upon
ourselves, rather than trusting you with all our hearts. We have
depended on our understanding, instead of seeking first your will.
We thought we saw the whole picture, but only a fraction was visible
to us. We assumed that we had adequate wisdom to make decisions
that were best, but our wisdom was faulty.

Gracious Father, we pray for your mercy and forgiveness for all
our sins of pride and for our failure to lean upon you for grace and
guidance.

O Lord, help us to acknowledge you as the Lord of our lives. We
do believe in you, and we pray that you will help us in our unbelief.

May you be the Lord of our thoughts and inner life.

May you be the Lord of our time.

May you be the Lord in our work.

May you be the Lord in our joys.

May you be the Lord in our illnesses and other misfortunes.

May you be the Lord in our joys.

May you be the Lord in the giving of our money and resources.

May you be the Lord in the use of our talents.

Thank you, Lord, for being our Lord. Amen.

Though the fig tree do not blossom,
nor fruit be on the vines,
the produce of the olive fail and the fields yield no food,
the flock be cut off from the fold and
there be no herd in the stalls,
yet I will rejoice in the Lord, I will joy in the God of
my salvation. God, the Lord, is my strength. . . .
Habakkuk 3:17–19

Sovereign Lord, we thank you for the faith of the prophet Habakkuk. In the face of insurmountable odds, he saw life through the lens of your steadfast love and unlimited grace. In the midst of his emptiness, he saw the fullness of your steadfast love. In the absence of material possessions, he rejoiced in the Lord. In his weakness, he knew the strength that comes from you alone.

Holy Father, in our heart of hearts we pray:

That over against our losses, we will see our gain in you,

That over against our pessimism, we will know the optimism of your grace,

That over against our temporality, we will feel the touch of the eternal,

That over against our weakness, we will be filled with the abundance of your transcendent power,

That over against our hopelessness, we will know true hope in Christ,

That over against our darkness, we will experience the dawn of eternal light,

That over against our being pushed for time, you will fill our time with the nearness of your presence, you who are the Alpha and the Omega, the beginning and the end. Amen.

Behold, he whose soul is not upright in him shall fail,
but the righteous shall live by his faith.
Habakkuk 2:4

O Lord our God, we confess our need of faith for our souls, just as we need breath for our bodies. As you breathed into us the breath of life at birth and provide continued breath for our bodies, we pray for continued faith.

Gracious God, strengthen our faith with a closer walk with you. Grant us the grace to be obedient to your call today.

Open our eyes of faith that we may see more clearly the truth of your Word and the light of your way.

Open our hearts by your love that we will be more receptive to your daily claims upon our lives.

Open our minds to the truth of your Word, and strengthen our wills to be doers of the Word.

Strengthen our hands in reaching out to the needy.

O Lord, we pray for your mercy and forgiveness when our faith has weakened though it might have been strong and courageous by your Spirit. Forgive us when we have clung to ourselves, rather than fling ourselves in utter trust into your arms of mercy.

Dear Master, we praise your name for those whose faith has inspired and stimulated us to grow in the formation of our faith.

We thank you for a little child's simple faith as he or she reached out with uplifted hands, and said, "Take me." Give us such willing hearts, O Christ, to be taken up by you. Amen.

... Faith working through love. ...
through love be servants of one another.
Galatians 5:6, 13

Eternal God, our Father, we praise your name for your love
that we have felt and seen working through the faith and love of
others. We are glad that space and time are not barriers of your
love, and neither are class or nationality. As we scan the horizons
of history, we meet those in whom we have seen faith working
through love. We realize we are surrounded by a great host of
witnesses. Their faith and acts of love continue to speak to us.
People like Abel, who "offered to God a more acceptable sacrifice
than Cain. . . . he died, but through faith he is still speaking"
(Heb.11:4).

We pray for the strengthening of our faith so that it will be
expressed through greater love and service in your name for others.
Enlighten our minds and soften our hearts with compassion to share
the burdens and sufferings of others.

O Lord, help us to see and understand our roles in life more in
terms of serving others than of being served. Grant that our faith,
expressed in love and service, will help to make the world a better
place for generations after us.

Dear Master, we believe that faith and love belong together.
Faith without works of love is no faith. Fill us with your faith so that
all we do will spring from hearts overflowing with that grace and
love. Amen.

Besides all these, taking the shield of faith, with which you
can quench all the flaming darts of the evil one.
Ephesians 6:16

Loving God, we thank you for the shield of faith, and we pray that our faith may not be weakened by neglect or by compromise. Deepen the channels of our faith. Strengthen our faith as we pass through difficult times. Help us to grow in our faith as we search the Scriptures. Open our eyes of faith in a clearer way that we may see your hand at work in our lives and in the lives of others.

We thank you, O Lord, for the blessings that come to us because of the faith of others, whose shield of faith is bright and shining.

O Christ, the Head of the church, our hearts are filled with gratitude for the building up of our faith through the fellowship of the church, where we hear the Word preached, share in Holy Communion, and join in the prayers, hymns of praise, and witness of the family of faith.

Continue your blessings, O Lord, upon your church, that she will so lift up Christ that others will be drawn unto Him. Lead each congregation into deeper commitments and wider service in the spirit of Christ.

We pray for those whose minds may be filled with doubts. Bind up also the brokenhearted. Forgive our sins, and restore unto us the joy of your salvation. May the blessedness of your presence be felt now by all who join us in prayer in the name of Jesus. Amen.

One who heard us was a woman named Lydia,
from the city of Thyatira, a seller of purple goods,
who was a worshiper of God.
The Lord opened her heart to give heed
to what was said by Paul.
. . . she was baptized, with her household. . . .
Acts 16:14–15

God of Light, we thank you for Lydia, whose heart was opened by your grace to hear and heed the gospel preached by Paul. We rejoice in her baptism and that of her household. Down through the centuries, Lydia's faith has continued to challenge others to believe.

We pray that our hearts will be open to heed the gospel that is proclaimed in our hearing, the gospel that confronts us in the Bible. Thank you, Lord, for the truth of what we hear proclaimed in the Bible, from the pulpit, in Christian writing, in the witness of believers, in the media, and in so many ways.

O Lord, may our minds and hearts be immersed in the truth of your Word. Grant that before we react in our human situations, we will first open our hearts to the action of your Word. May your Spirit so master our spirits that our attitudes and relations with others will express the mind of Christ. Grant that your Word will become so incarnate in us that our words and deeds will bear witness to Christ.

Lord God, we pray that you will raise up a host of other Lydias, who will witness to their faith in Christ with hospitality and caring to spread the gospel of Christ near and far. Amen.

Teach me thy way, O Lord,
that I may walk in thy truth.
Psalm 86:11

Dear Master and Teacher, we confess our need to be taught by you. We need to see, with our eyes of faith and the understanding of our hearts, the truth of your Word. We are too close to ourselves to truly know who we are, but you know us altogether. Clarify our vision of your way, O Lord, and empower us to walk steadfastly in your paths. Help us to see clearly your way in our complex world of many ways. We pray for discerning minds and perceptive hearts to know the direction of your will and for the grace to do it.

Help us, O Lord, to stop and to look and listen for your Word that comes to us in reading the Scriptures, prayer, and worship. We know that you are present. Help us to be present with open minds, listening ears, and eager hearts of faith to hear with a will to do your bidding.

We lift our hearts in gratitude for your providential care. Guide and keep us this day. Direct our thoughts, words, and actions. As we touch the lives of others, be our Mediator and unite us in the Spirit. Go ahead of us to prepare us and those we meet to encourage each other in our journey of faith.

We pray for the forgiveness of our sins and our faltering steps. May we give our "Yes" to you in obedience. In the name of Christ our Lord we ask this. Amen.

And it came to pass,
when the time was come
that he should be received up,
he steadfastly set his face to go to Jerusalem.
Luke 9:51 (KJV)

Our Father God, we lift our hearts in humble gratitude for the coming of Jesus Christ into the world to redeem the world from sin. We thank you that Jesus steadfastly set his face to go to Jerusalem, and there was no turning back from the Cross because of his obedience to your will.

We pray for grace that we may be as resolute in turning to Christ as he was in going to Jerusalem.

We pray for your grace to overcome our pride. May our hearts be open to accept all that Christ has done for us at Calvary. May we not try to prove our righteousness, but be clothed in his righteousness.

We thank you, O Lord, that it is by the brokenness of Christ that our own brokenness is healed. He is our "Wounded Healer," who binds up our wounds by his love and redeeming grace.

We pray today for those who suffer in mind, body, and spirit. Some are burdened with anxiety, wondering what really lies ahead of them in illness. Some need the good that only Christ can give. There are some who are lonely and feel that no one really cares for them. In all of our human situations, loving God, we pray for the guidance and strength of the Holy Spirit. Surround us, O Lord, with your presence. Use us in some way today to witness to your love in Christ. Amen.

For with God, nothing will be impossible.
Luke 1:37

O Lord, you are from everlasting to everlasting; and so today we praise your name for your mighty deeds of the past. Just as in creation you said, "Let there be light," and there was light, so still today you have the power to speak and it is done.

Forgive us, O God, when we have failed to broaden and deepen our understanding of your grace and power. Too often, in our limited vision and little faith, we have failed to consider what you could do in and through us. We have assumed that we can do all that can be done in situations, rather than seeing the greater possibilities that divine strength makes possible.

Holy Father, you know what faces us today. We pray that you will preserve our going out and coming in. Surround us with your providential care.

O Holy Spirit, so fill our hearts with your light and power that we will see your hand at work in our lives, transforming what we see as impossible, and making it possible by your grace.

Heal the brokenness of our lives.

Bind up our broken relations transforming our alienations from others and from you, O Lord, by the reconciliation of your grace.

We pray for those whose hearts are grieving. Comfort them with your divine presence. Help them to see in the midst of darkness the light that only Jesus Christ can bring.

Grant, O Lord, that the words of Paul, "I can do all things through Christ, who strengthens me," will become our faith also, through Christ our Lord. Amen.

O God, thou art my God; early will I seek thee;
my soul thirsteth for thee. . . .
Psalm 63:1 (KJV)

Our Father God, there are so many tasks before me today that I need even more time to be alone in your presence. What is before me is greater than my strength and wisdom. In this day as my life touches others, may there also be an intersection of the Eternal One. I call upon you, O Lord, for a sense of your abiding presence through the day. Cleanse my heart and mind from sinful desires and selfish thoughts.

Go ahead of me in the hours and events of the day in such a way that I may see your hand at work in me and in those with whom I live and work.

O Lord, this day, as every day, is a gift from your hand. I would not pray only for myself. Grant all who pray the faith to see the experiences of the day in the light of your will. Help us to see the persons we encounter as precious in your sight, and those for whom Christ died to save.

When problems arise, we pray for your power and wisdom in dealing with them. When decisions are to be made, may we have the inward witness of the Holy Spirit guiding us. As we set sail on the sea of life early in the morning, O Lord, we are trusting in the winds of your Spirit to move us forward in living this day for you. We do not know what the day holds for us, but the time for trusting in you and serving you is always present. In that spirit, we go forth today to live for you in the name of Christ. Amen.

Seek the Lord while he may be found,
and call upon him while he is near.
Isaiah 55:6

When you search for me, you will find me;
if you seek me with all your heart.
Jeremiah 29:13 (NRSV)

O Lord, we confess that at times you seem far removed from us, and we wonder if you are present. Yet in our hearts, we know that you have not forsaken us; it is we who have left you in our pride, our self-centered round of activities, and our interests.

In such moments, O Father, we turn to you in faith that you are near. Grant us the grace to seek you with all our hearts. We know that you find us even before we turn to you. We lift our hearts in praise for your long, strong arm and strong hand that reach out after us wherever we are in thought, desire, or place. Our hearts sing for joy in your presence.

Gracious God, we pray for your abiding presence to be with us through the experiences of this day and night. You know what lies ahead of us, including the persons we will meet who are related to us in one way or another. Help us in whatever situations surround us, to respond in the light and power of your Word, to hear your call and answer in faith and obedience.

Creator God, we pray that our eyes will be open to see your nearness in the world about us. In the faces of friends and strangers, may we see the result of the touch of your hand upon them. Lord, forbid that we pass by on the other side from anyone to whom we might give a helping hand.

Thank you for being our Good Shepherd, searching and finding us in love. May our response be with our whole hearts in the spirit of Jesus. Amen.

Jesus said to them, "Children, have you any fish?"
They answered, "No." He said to them, "Cast the net on
the right side of the boat, and you will find some."
So they cast it, and now they were not able to haul it in,
for the quantity of fish.
John 21:5–6

Eternal God, we pray for those who have pulled up the net of their lives and found emptiness, meaninglessness. We pray that they will cast their net "on the right side" with Christ, who can fill all activities with meaning and purpose and the joy of the abundant life.

When we are impatient about what others should do for us, help us "to cast our net" on the right side by helping someone else in need.

When we are burdened with guilt over the things we should not have done and the things we should have done but failed to do, grant us the grace to cast our nets "on the right side" of God's promises of forgiveness and redeeming love.

When life is overburdened with cares and anxiety, enable us to cast the net of our cares "on the right side" of God's infinite care. Help us to trust him, leaving the results in his hands.

When we have cast our net of life out primarily to gain material things which perish, we pray for grace to cast life "on the right side" for God's eternal things that do not perish.

Patient Lord, help us today to sit down beside some lonely person to listen quietly as burdens are shared, that we may help make their burdens lighter.

Forgive us, O Lord, when we have been set on doing our will; grant us grace to cast our desires "on the right side" at Jesus' command, that we may know the abundance of his joy and peace. We make our prayer in Jesus' name. Amen.

21

CONFESSION

*If we say we have no sin, we deceive ourselves,
and the truth is not in us. If we confess our sins,
he is faithful and just, and will forgive our sins
and cleanse us from all unrighteousness.*
1 John 1:8–9

O Lord our God, because we know that you are acquainted with all our ways, and that no secrets are hidden from you, we confess that we stand in need of your mercy. We thank you, Gracious God, for the promise that if we confess our sins, you will forgive us, cleanse our hearts, and set us free in your grace.

We do confess our sins and our need of your forgiveness.

We confess our weakness and our need of strength of soul that you alone can supply.

We confess our inadequacy for life and our need of your sufficiency.

We confess that our burdens are greater than we can bear, and that we need the "blessed burden that makes all burdens light."

We confess our brokenness of heart and our need of the binding up that comes alone from the Crucified.

We confess our need of the guidance of the Holy Spirit, that our feet may walk in the paths of your righteousness.

O Lord, we praise your name for your forgiving grace. Send us forth in this day to live in faith and obedience in the name of Christ. Amen.

Say to them, As I live, says the Lord God,
I have no pleasure in the death of the wicked, but that
the wicked turn from his way and live; turn back,
turn back from your evil ways; for why will you die,
O house of Israel?
Ezekiel 33:11

Lord God, we are glad that you do not take pleasure in the death of the wicked. This helps free us to confess the wickedness of our own hearts and to pray for your mercy and forgiveness. We pray that you will:

Cast out the pride that makes us feel sufficient within ourselves,

Cleanse our hearts of self-seeking, and create a spirit of self-giving love,

Enable us by the power of your Holy Spirit to turn from our sins of thought, word, and deed and to know the joy of your salvation.

As we go through the experiences of this day, help us to praise your name for life. We pray that our work will be acceptable in your sight: our travel blessed with your divine providence, our recreation with renewal, our suffering with victory, our decisions with wisdom, our study with understanding, and our social relations with appreciation for others.

O Everlasting God, may the light of your countenance fall upon our swiftly passing days. Let the light of your everlasting love pierce the depths of our hearts. May the warmth of your compassion soften our hearts. Grant that the light of your glory will shine upon our paths through Christ our Lord. Amen.

And they heard the sound of the Lord God
walking in the garden in the cool of the day,
and the man and his wife hid themselves
from the presence of the Lord God
among the trees of the garden.
Genesis 3:8

O Lord God, as Adam and Eve sought to hide from you because of their disobedience in eating the forbidden fruit, so we too, ashamed of our sin, have also tried to hide from your presence.

We have hidden under the burden of our guilt.

We have hidden under an avalanche of activities, some of them noble.

We have hidden under our moral deeds, thinking they were sufficient to cover our sins.

We have hidden under the demands of others.

We have hidden under a tight schedule.

We have hidden under health problems, handicaps, and various situations.

We have hidden, not realizing you were inescapable.

We have hidden behind someone else's faults—or their goodness.

We have hidden under the canopy of the church.

O Lord, we know better, and there is no hiding from you, for you are there at the turn of every corner. We pray for your forgiveness for our seeking to evade you. Grant us the grace to turn our lives over to you, trusting in your mercy and forgiving love in the name of Christ. Amen.

Confess your faults one to another,
and pray one for another, that you may be healed.
The effectual fervent prayer of a righteous man
availeth much.
James 5:16 (KJV)

Our Father God, we admit that it is easier to confess
another's faults than it is to see and confess our own. Help us to
remember that when we are critical of another's faults, it may be
that we are directing attention to someone else to avoid facing our
own weaknesses.

Help us to pray for one another and to pray especially for those
who have wronged us. Grant us a spirit of forgiveness and understanding. May these and all our prayers be true prayers—ones in
which your Holy Spirit prompts our praying.

We lift our hearts in praise and thanksgiving for all your blessings.
As we count our blessings, we find they are more than we can
number.

Regardless of what others do, give us the courage and faith to
commit our lives to you, O Lord. May others be encouraged by our
steadfast commitment.

We pray for those who join us now in prayer. Touch each heart
with your love and meet every need. Help us to know the all-
sufficiency of Christ.

All powerful God, we pray that our prayers of intercession for
one another will be prompted by the Holy Spirit—that our prayers
will rise from hearts possessed by the Spirit—that our prayers will
avail by your grace as we bring them in the name of Christ. Amen.

22

FORGIVENESS

Search me, O God and know my heart!
Try me and know my thoughts!
And see if there be any wicked way in me,
And lead me in the way everlasting.
Psalm 139:23–24

Keep your heart with all vigilance;
for from it flow the springs of life. . .
Take heed to the path of your feet,
then all your ways will be sure.
Proverbs 4:23, 26

O Lord our God, you know the secrets of our hearts—our thoughts, motives, and desires—and you are acquainted with all our ways. We pray for wisdom and grace to examine our ways. Forgive us when we have sought to justify our actions when we should have confessed our wrongs and repented of our sins. Create within us clean hearts, and restore a right spirit that we may glorify you. Make our love for you, O Lord, as steadfast as your love is for us. Enable us by your grace to keep our covenant with you as you keep your covenant with us.

Lift our horizons from the shadows of earth that we may see eternal things and seek first your Kingdom, O God, and your right-eousness. Amid the uncertainties of life, may we go forth in the certainty of your steadfast love and abiding presence. In the name of Christ we pray. Amen.

Why do you see the speck that is in your brother's eye,
but do not notice the log that is in your own eye?
Luke 6:41

O Lord, grant that we will be less concerned about the flaws of others and more aware of our own weaknesses. Sharpen our perceptions to see the good in others. Make us quick to encourage them and slow to criticize. Enable us to see persons through the tender and compassionate eyes of Christ.

Gracious God, we pray that even our prayers for others will not be a means of deflecting the searchlight of the Spirit from revealing the sin of our own hearts. Help us to be honest with ourselves in the light of your grace. Take away the blindness that keeps us from seeing the impurities of our motives. Grant us a spirit of true repentance for our sins and the faith to cast ourselves upon your mercy, trusting and receiving your forgiveness. Bathe us with the warmth of your love. Surround us with your providential care. Lift us up and send us forth to walk in your holy ways.

We are grateful, O Lord, that you have not made us to be puppets but persons who image you in our workaday world. Open our eyes to see the opportunities in which we may share your love and caring with others. May we not be blinded by the temptation to wait for some great distant moment to serve you, when each new day brings unprecedented opportunities to be channels of your grace.

O Christ, may your light shine through us today in some way to encourage another in that person's journey of faith. Amen.

> Then they seized him and led him away,
> bringing him into the high priest's house.
> Peter followed at a distance. . . .
> Then a maid said . . . "This man also was with him."
> But he denied it.
> Luke 22:54, 56

Lord Jesus, too often we see ourselves in Peter's following at a distance, while his denial is reflected in our own hearts. We confess that we have followed you at a distance. The tensions and stress of daily things have come in-between us. We have listened to other voices calling us. We have marched to a different drummer than you. We have let our fears control us, rather than trusting in your Word. We have been absorbed with other things and with ourselves. We know that you have not forsaken us, but it is we who have turned aside from the light and glory of your presence.

Blessed Lord, we pray for your mercy and the forgiveness for our sins. We want the sense of your presence and the peace you give more than anything in the world. We want to be flooded with your grace in the depths of our hearts.

Father God, we believe the promise of your Word, that if we draw near to you, you will draw near to us. We need your grace that will enable us to draw near to you. As we reach out to you today, help us to feel the touch of your hand upon us, directing, prodding, comforting, and reassuring. Then open our eyes to the needs of someone else and use us to help meet their needs through Christ our Lord. Amen.

Jesus, once more deeply moved, came to the tomb.
It was a cave with a stone laid across the entrance.
"Take away the stone," he said.
John 11:38–39 (NIV)

O Lord, as you came to Lazarus's tomb and said, "Take away the stone," we beseech you to come to us and take away all that stands between us and you.

Take away our sins and the guilt of our conscience, and grant us the joy of your salvation.

Take away the dimness of our souls, that we may see the glory of your presence.

Take away the dullness of our minds, and sharpen our understanding of your Word for us.

Take away the stubbornness of our wills, and make us steadfast in doing your will.

Take away the lukewarmness of our faith, and quicken our zeal as disciples of Jesus Christ.

Take us out of the shallow waters of religiosity, and launch us out into the depths of your grace.

Take away the anxieties that perplex us, and grant us the gift of your peace.

Take away our fears of what may happen in the future, and help us to put our trust in you, O Lord, without reservations.

O Christ, enable us by your grace to take our hands off of ourselves and to place our lives firmly in the grip of your hands. Amen.

23

SUFFERING

I consider that the sufferings of this present time
are not worth comparing with the glory
that is to be revealed in us.
Romans 8:18

O God, you who are the source of all life and the lover of all persons, we thank you for your presence with us in our sufferings. We rejoice that you know, better than we, what we are going through in our times of hurt and crisis.

It is our prayer, O Lord, that you will make our sufferings redemptive for us and for all who are touched by our pain. We believe that you can do for us what we cannot do for ourselves, bringing good out of times of trial. Flow through our minds and hearts, O Holy Spirit, to wash away any spirit of resentment or self-pity. Forgive us when we have been self-centered. Grant us peace in the wonder of your love, forgiveness, and comfort.

In the light of your wisdom, Gracious God, enable us to see beyond today's trials to the dawn of a new day in your providential care. Help us to see that our pain and agony at this time cannot be compared with the glory that will be ours in Christ Jesus. So fill our hearts with your love that we will see your hand at work, bringing to pass that which is good and pleasing in your sight. We pray for the patience and grace to know and accept your timing and will in our suffering. We pray that in the darkest hours of our pain, the light and glory of your presence will shine through, keeping us on course with the Comforter. Amen.

For he was looking forward to the city with foundations,
whose architect and builder is God.
Hebrews 11:10 (NIV)

But our citizenship is in heaven.
Philippians 3:20 (NIV)

Eternal God, Lord of Heaven and Earth, our soul is flooded with your mercies. You created us in your image and placed us on earth to live a heavenly life by your grace. O Lord, we bless you for the wonder of our creation, and praise you that in our earthly journey of faith we may taste "the powers of the world to come."

We thank you, Lord, for creating us for earth and for heaven. Open our eyes to see the eternal significance of our earthly tasks, and grant us the presence of your Holy Spirit that empowers us to be faithful servants.

In our going and coming in the routine of daily life, in the performance of our work, and in our associations with others we beseech thee, O Lord, to use us to reflect something of the love and truth of Christ. May it be apparent to others that we belong to you, that we are your children.

We pray for those who have only an earthly sense of direction in life, for those whose lives are just filled with "stuff," for those whose hearts ache with a great void, and for those whose lives are in bondage to drugs or alcohol addiction. Gracious God, encircle with your everlasting arms of divine comfort those who are passing through some tunnel of suffering and sorrow. Grant that all will find the path of true life in the steadfast love of the Lord. Amen.

Prepare to meet your God, O Israel.
Amos 4:12

Thus saith the Lord, Set thine house in order;
for thou shalt die, and not live.
2 Kings 20:1 (KJV)

Almighty and merciful God, we confess that we need your mercy and grace to set our houses in order to meet you. We confess that we have sinned against you in thought, word, and deed. We are grieved by the evil that we failed to turn away from, and we have seen the good that we should have done, but failed to do.

Gracious God, grant us true repentance for our sins, and the grace to trust your promise, that "if we confess our sins, [you are] faithful and just and will forgive us our sins and purify us from all unrighteousness" (1 John 1:9 NIV).

O Lord, we believe that when our lives are in your hands they are in safekeeping for all time and in the world to come. Forgive us when we thought we would prepare to meet you by our own patching up with some good deeds. Help us, loving God, to live each day in the light of your presence and with the power of your Holy Spirit.

Lord, we believe that the best preparation to meet you in death, and in eternity, is to live life with you today. We thank you for the peace-giving hope we have in Christ that we will meet you, Lord, clothed in your righteousness.

"Eternal God, who committest to us the swift and solemn trust of life. Since we know not what a day may bring forth, but only that the hour for serving thee is always present, may we wake to the instant claims of thy holy will, not waiting for tomorrow, but yielding today."[†] As we have trusted you in this life, keep us in your love and care in the world to come through Jesus Christ our Lord. Amen.

[†]*Ritual of the United Methodist Church,* (Nashville, Tenn.: United Methodist Publishing House, 1964), 45.

In those days Hezekiah became sick and was at the point of death. And Isaiah the prophet the son of Amoz came to him, and said to him, "Thus says the Lord, 'Set your house in order; for you shall die, you shall not recover.'"
2 Kings 20:1

Almighty God, by your mercies you have created us and given us the days of our lives. As we approach the time of our departure from this life, whether soon or later, we confess our sins and failures to live life wholly and fully for you. We pray for your mercy and the forgiveness of all our sins.

Forgive us, O Lord:

When we have wronged others,

When we had an unforgiving spirit toward another,

When our words brought pain to another,

When our relationships with family or friends resulted in alienation and separation rather than reconciliation and love,

When we held a grudge against someone,

When we failed to do the good we knew,

When we judged another rather than seeing our own sin and failure,

When we expected more of others than of ourselves,

When we were self-centered, rather than trusting you, Lord, for guidance and strength.

O Lord, strip away our "righteousness," and clothe us with the righteousness of Christ by faith. Thus may our lives be in order whenever the time of our death comes. In Jesus' name we pray. Amen.

I kept my faith, even when I said,
"I am greatly afflicted. . . ."
Precious in the sight of the Lord is
the death of his saints.
Psalm 116:10, 15

O merciful Lord, in the midst of our loss and sorrow, your grace and light shine through our grief. We are not the only ones who know the pain in the death of a loved one. Yet our grief touches us in a way that we have never before experienced.

We thank you, Lord, for those who have kept the faith in the midst of their afflictions and loss. Strengthen our faith as we walk life's paths unaccompanied by a dear one who has gone ahead of us to the Father's house.

"So teach us to number our days, that we may gain a heart of wisdom," and live our lives in the center of your will.

Gracious God, we pray for your everlasting arms to surround, comfort, and strengthen all who are in sorrow. Dear Master, you who are a "man of sorrow and acquainted with grief," help us to bear our pain and sorrow in the same spirit that you bore yours.

Eternal God our Father, grant that we may so live that our death will be precious in your sight. In Jesus' name. Amen.

. . . call upon me in the day of trouble; I will deliver you,
and you shall glorify me.
Psalm 50:15

O Lord, our Good Shepherd, we thank you for being with us in times of crisis and trouble. Your presence makes all the difference in our world. The light of your presence enables us to see through the shadows. Heavenly Father, we believe the words of your Son who said, "I am the light of the world; he who follows me will not walk in darkness, but will have the light of life" (John 8:12). We pray for your grace to walk in His light.

Dear Lord, since we do not know what this day holds for us, but only that it is another day in which to serve you, empower us by your Holy Spirit:

To walk into the shadows with faith in the Light that shines through the shadows,

To look to you, Lord, for the help that you alone can give,

To see another's pain and suffering and do something to make that person's burdens lighter,

To believe in your promise that you are at work in everything for the good of those who love you, who are called according to your purpose.

Thank you, Lord, for the inspiration and encouragement that comes to us as we see others meeting their trials victoriously through your grace. Deliver us from self-pity; cast out our sin of rebellion and blaming you, and grant us grace to glorify you in Jesus' name. Amen.

Bear one another's burdens, and so fulfill the law of Christ.
. . . for each man will have to bear his own load.
Galatians 6:2, 5

O Lord our God and Creator, sometimes life seems to come wrapped in burdens and problems. For some it appears that as soon as they overcome one obstacle, another is waiting for them. We pray for the wisdom and will to see below the surface of others and to sense something of the loads they are carrying.

Gracious Lord, give us wise and encouraging words to say, and show us the time to reach out with a helping hand to make another's burden lighter.

Deepen our awareness, because in a sense, all of us must carry our own loads. No one else can get inside of us and do for us what we must do. But you can be with us, O Lord, and that makes our burden lighter and dispels our anxiety. Forgive us when we have complained about our load.

We pray that we may so bear our burdens and carry our loads that we may be a source of inspiration and strength for others. Grant us patience and quiet strength when the pressures, tensions, sorrows, and anxieties come our way.

Caring God, fulfill in our lives your promise that in everything God works for the good of those who love him, who are called according to his purpose (Rom. 8:28). So fill our hearts with your love that we may see your hand at work in our lives and in the lives of others, bringing to pass that which is pleasing in your sight. Grant that our present afflictions will prepare us for an eternal glory in the world to come, through Christ our Lord. Amen.

24

SERVANTHOOD

I am among you as one who serves.
Luke 22:27

O Christ, you walked in the lowly paths of Palestine, bearing witness to God's redeeming love. Wherever you went you left your footprints of service for others. Others came to know God because of your self-giving love.

Dear Master, in whose life we see what we yearn to be, we lift our hearts in praise for your life, service, death on the Cross, and resurrection. Through them we may truly know the joy of salvation in your name.

O Lord, when we ponder the meaning of what you have done for us, our hearts are humbled. We thank you for your call to us to come and follow you.

Amid the perplexities and uncertainties of our world, may our ears be attentive to your voice, our minds open to your truth, and our hearts responsive to your will. Grant us the grace and power of your Holy Spirit that we may walk in your ways of service.

Open our eyes to see the opportunities that unfold today to serve you. Help us to make someone else's burden lighter. Reach out through us to make your will known. May our words be the channel of your Word spoken to someone in need of the message that you alone can speak.

O Holy Spirit of God, cast out of our minds and hearts any self-seeking or self-serving desires, or any hidden desire to be served. Rather, fill our hearts with the Spirit of him who came to serve. Amen.

... whoever would be great among you must be your
servant, . . . For the Son of man also came not to be served
but to serve, and to give his life as a ransom for many.
Mark 10:43, 45

Our Father God, Jesus always lifts before us the highest
ideals and the noblest way of life. We confess that we have not
always looked to those ideals nor followed his way. Too often our
selfishness and pride have eclipsed his ideals, and our feet have
walked in another way. Instead of seeking to serve others, we have
had in mind how others might serve us—what they might do for us.
We have been more concerned about our status with those "above"
us than with serving those around us.

O Lord our God, we pray that your mercy, grace, and forgiveness
will so transform our lives that they will be turned outward to see
and reach out in a true spirit of servanthood to others. May our lives
be measured not in terms of what we have gained or what has come
to us, but in what we have given and shared with others in the love
of Christ.

Open our *eyes* to see how and where we may serve others in the
spirit of Christ.

Open our *ears* to hear the cries of those in need, and teach us to
respond in a Christlike spirit.

Gracious Lord, grant us the grace to abandon ourselves to your
will and way, that our spirit of service and our deeds will express the
mind and heart of the Crucified. Amen.

Abide in me, and I in you. As the branch cannot bear fruit
by itself, unless it abides in the vine, neither can you,
unless you abide in me.
I am the vine, you are the branches.
He who abides in me, and I in him, he it is that bears
much fruit, for apart from me you can do nothing.

John 15:4–5

Blessed Lord, help us to grow in our understanding of what it means to abide in you, because we want our lives to be fruitful in the things of the Spirit. Surely, to abide in you and for you to abide in us means:

For us to put our utter trust in you,

For us to know your abiding presence,

For us to be open to the directions of your Holy Spirit,

For us to know the joy that you alone can give,

For us to have in our hearts your peace, that the world can neither give nor take from us,

For us to be filled with faith and hope as we await whatever lies before us in the future,

For us to be more concerned with the spiritual dimensions than the material aspects of life,

For us to be bearing fruit in the Kingdom of God because of your grace, and

For us to taste the powers of the world to come.

Forgive us, O Lord, when we have tried to go it alone without you. We pray that you will forgive our failure to abide in you and bear much fruit. Transform our lives by your grace for greater fruitfulness through Christ our Savior. Amen.

25
WORSHIP

Come, let us go up to the mountain of the Lord, to the
house of the God of Jacob; that he may teach us his ways
and that we may walk in his paths.
Micah 4:2

O holy and righteous God, we thank you for the call to go to
your house and worship you. We thank you for the deep desires and
longings of our hearts that can only be satisfied in your presence and
by your grace. We thank you for your house which has a special
meaning for us, because there you have met our deepest need so
many times in the hours of worship.

In your house we have been taught your Word and ways.

In your house we have seen your image reflected in the lives of
fellow pilgrims of the faith.

In your house we have lifted our prayers and praise.

In your house we have heard your gospel of salvation and
eternal life proclaimed.

In your house your Spirit has convicted us of sin and brought us
new life in Christ.

In your house we have found comfort, strength, and hope in our
journey of faith.

In your house we have been strengthened by the bonds of
Christian love and fellowship.

In your house we have found life's ultimate meaning and the
grace to walk in your paths.

In your house our lives have been transformed and renewed by
the power of the Holy Spirit.

Enable us, O Lord, to go forth to serve you in the same spirit
that you call us to worship. Amen.

Remember the sabbath day, to keep it holy.
Exodus 20:8

Enter his gates with thanksgiving,
and his courts with praise!
Give thanks to him, bless his name!
Psalm 100:4

Eternal God our Father, we thank you for the commandment to keep the Sabbath holy—a day of rest, worship, and renewal—a day that gives meaning to all other days. We are grateful that as Christians we join the observance of the Sabbath with the celebration of the resurrection of Jesus Christ from the dead on the first day of the week.

Lord God, who rested on the seventh day after creating the world, help us to see our need for rest from our work. In keeping the Sabbath, we reaffirm our dependence upon you and our trust in you, Lord.

We pray that as we worship we may release our grip on our lives so that you may grip them more firmly by your divine power.

O God, as you have promised to be present where two or three are gathered in your name, so help us to be present with open minds, listening ears, and eager hearts of faith to receive your Word. We pray for those who are unable to be a part of a congregation in worship on Sunday. We thank you that their private prayers and worship, as well as ours, are acceptable in your sight, O Lord our strength and Redeemer.

Gracious God, we thank you for your rich blessings upon us in worship on Sunday, for the renewal of our spiritual life for the week ahead. May we draw upon the strength we gain from worship throughout the week. We offer our prayer in the name of Christ our Lord. Amen.

How lovely is thy dwelling place, O Lord of hosts!
My soul longs, Yea, faints for the courts of the Lord;
my heart and flesh sing for joy to the living God.
Psalm 84:1–2

O Living Lord, how wonderful it is to be gathered together in your house to worship you! Our hearts are blessed every time we meet in your name because you are always present. As we greet family, friends, and visitors, the touch of their lives reminds us of your providential care and blessings. We thank you, O Lord, for the outreach of your grace that comes to us through them.

We pray for all pastors as they gather up in their prayers the prayers, burdens, and longings of their congregations. As they proclaim the gospel of Jesus Christ, may your Word be spoken to each listener. O God, prepare our hearts for your Word, and as that Word is spoken to us, open our minds and hearts to receive it and to act upon it. For those who have not believed, we also pray asking that as they hear the gospel, faith will come to them, and they will know the joy of your salvation.

Gracious Lord, we pray for your healing and comforting grace to engulf the brokenhearted and those who grieve. Grant the healing touch of Christ to those who suffer physical pain.

Be with those who are unable to worship in a gathered congregation on Sunday. Wherever they are, may their hearts also be lifted in prayer, praise, and genuine worship.

O Lord, help us to worship you in the beauty of holiness and in the power of your grace through faith in Christ our Redeemer. Amen.

I was glad when they said unto me,
Let us go to the house of the Lord!
Psalm 122:1

Our Father God, we join with the psalmist today in expressing the joy of going to your house for worship. We lift our hearts in praise and thanksgiving for the privilege of worship—that we have the freedom of worship. We pray for your Holy Spirit to be present in each service of worship. Wherever the family of God is gathered, may they worship in spirit and in truth. As we are gathered in your house for worship, O Lord, we pray that you will continue to teach us your ways and give us the grace to walk in your paths.

Send out your light on our pathway today that we may not stumble or fall away from the path that is right. Be in our thoughts. Speak through our words. Help us to be sensitive to the needs of others and to be aware of their true feelings.

May our relationships with our families and those beyond our families reflect a right relationship with you and with them. As Jesus said, "As you did it unto one of the least of these, you did it to me," grant us grace to treat other persons as we would treat Jesus. Deepen the channels of our compassion. Bless the ones who join us now in prayer. Speak to them the word they most need to hear.

We pray, Lord, that our worship may be an adventure of the heart—purifying, enlightening, and transforming our lives by the power of your Holy Spirit. May our souls be nourished in worship that we may glorify you, Lord, in life and in death. In the name of the Risen Christ we ask these things. Amen.

26

LISTENING

If you listen carefully to the voice of the Lord your God
and do what is right in his eyes, . . .
Exodus 15:26 (NIV)

Father God, as we come to your throne of grace today, we pray
that we may listen carefully to your Word for us.

That we may hear your Word distinctly.

That our minds will be attentive to your Word.

That we will fully understand your purpose for our lives in our
present situations.

That our hearts will be responsive to your Word.

That our wills will be obedient to your Spirit's prompting.

That our spirits will know the presence and power of your Holy
Spirit bearing witness with our spirits that we are yours.

O Lord, we confess that often we have not listened carefully to
your voice. We have not been still enough to listen. Instead, we
have rushed out into the day as though we were sufficient within
ourselves for whatever the day might bring. Have mercy upon us, O
God, and forgive our sins of pride, haste, and indifference.

We pray for the grace and wisdom to lean upon your promises
and to put our trust fully in you.

Enable us by your grace to be not only hearers of your Word, but
also doers of the Word.

Since we do not know what situations we will encounter, we
pray that we will be responsive to your Spirit and obedient to your
will in the name and spirit of Christ. Amen.

> But they rebelled against me
> and would not listen to me.
> Ezekiel 20:8

O God of the ages, your Word to the people of Israel through the prophet Ezekiel speaks to us, for our hearts have also rebelled against you. We have been distraught in circumstances and blamed you or other persons for what has happened. We wondered why you did not step in to give us a quick and easy answer.

Heavenly Father, time and time again we have not been willing to really listen to you. The voices around us, the cries of our own hearts, the anxieties of our minds, and the stubbornness of our wills have deafened us to your voice. We have been more anxious to speak than to listen, especially to listen to you, Lord.

Gracious God, we pray for the forgiveness of our sins whether of rebellion or of unwillingness to listen to your call and claim upon our lives. May we learn to listen for your Word that speaks to us through the Scriptures, through other persons, and through circumstances and events of the day.

Lord God, quicken our awareness of your presence in the midst of our daily living. Remind us that you have a way of speaking in unexpected places, through surprising persons, and in unconventional forms. Cast out the blindness of our souls so that we will be listening for you at the turn of every corner of our lives. We offer our prayer in the name of Jesus our Savior. Amen.

I waited patiently for the Lord;
he inclined to me and heard my cry.
Psalm 40:1

Our Father God, we confess our impatience. Too often we have failed to wait for your coming. We have tried to tell you what we want, rather than listening to what you demand of us. We pray you will forgive us for seeking to set the agenda for our lives without consulting you first.

O Lord, how patient you have been with us as again and again we have failed you in our thoughts, words, and deeds! We pray for your mercy and the forgiveness of our sins. Cleanse our hearts, and set us free in your redeeming grace.

Holy father, we thank you that you do hear the cries of our hearts. We believe that you are even more aware of our needs than we.

We thank you for the comfort of your divine presence as we cry out in agony of spirit.

We thank you for wiping our tears and causing us to see the sunny side of life.

We thank you for giving us another chance.

We thank you for your everlasting arms that surround and support us.

We thank you for Jesus Christ, who is the Way, the Truth, and the Life.

We thank you for our daily bread and all the necessities of life.

O Lord, make us the instruments of your hand to be a blessing to others in need, whether they are nearby or far away. Amen.

27

TIME

My times are in thy hand.
Psalm 31:15

In all your ways acknowledge him,
and he will make straight your paths.
Proverbs 3:6

O God our Father, you are the Creator of our lives and of time itself. It was you who called us into being in our time. We thank you for life and for the times in which we live. We pray you will "So teach us to number our days that we may get a heart of wisdom" (Ps. 90:12) and live our lives fully for you.

Gracious God, we pray that our times and our lives will truly be in your hands. We confess that often we have sought to be our own pilots. Grant us forgiveness for our sins of pride in refusing to trust you with all that we have and are. Help us to learn anew that where you guide, you provide.

"Eternal God, who committest to us the swift and solemn trust of life: Since we know not what a day may bring forth, but only that the hour for serving thee is always present, may we wake to the instant claims of thy holy will, not waiting for tomorrow, but yielding today. Consecrate with thy presence the way our feet may go; and the humblest work will shine and the roughest places be made plain."[†]

God of Light, who has shone upon us in the past, we lift our praise and thanksgiving. Into the unknown we go with confidence

---

[†]*Ritual of the United Methodist Church*, (Nashville, Tenn.: United Methodist Publishing House, 1964), 45.

and hope because of your steadfast love. We pray that whatever meets us in the future, we shall face it in your strength and with the consciousness of your abiding presence through Christ our Lord. Amen.

> The Lord said to Moses and Aaron in Egypt,
> "This month is to be for you the first month, the first
> month of your year . . . on the tenth day of this month
> each man is to take a lamb for his family."
> Exodus 12:1–3 (NIV)

O Lord, God of all time, we thank you for your wisdom in timing. Help us to see that your planning for events and experiences in our lives is best, just as it was when long ago, the time came to deliver the children of Israel from their bondage under Pharaoh. Likewise, "when the time had fully come you sent forth your Son" (Gal. 4:4) "that whoever believes in him should not perish but have eternal life" (John 3:6).

Gracious God, so fill our hearts with the abiding presence of your Holy Spirit that we may see your hand at work, bringing to pass that which is pleasing in your sight. Deliver us from our bondage to sin and fear, and set us free in your redeeming grace. Help us to fill the hours of each day with deeds of love and service in your holy name. Open our eyes to the sufferings of others, and help us to make their struggles easier.

Enable us, by your grace, to live life in harmony with your divine purpose with the passing of each day.

O Lord, forgive us if we have complained when your timing did not correspond to what we thought was the right time. Help us to realize that you see the whole pattern, but we can view only a few threads in the whole garment of life. We pray that your purposes will be accomplished in our lives in the name of Christ. Amen.

The steadfast love of the Lord never ceases,
his mercies never come to an end;
they are new every morning; great is thy faithfulness.
Lamentations 3:22–23

This is the day which the Lord has made,
let us rejoice and be glad in it.
Psalm 118:24

O Lord our God, this day which you have made comes fresh from your hands. No one has ever seen it before, nor will anyone ever see it again. We thank you for the light of this day and pray for your presence and the guidance of your Holy Spirit as we live it. We are glad to be alive and to have some work to do in your name. We know that even when we are laid aside from the mainstream of life, we have a place to serve.

Holy Father, send us to someone, or send someone to us, with whom we might share what Christ has done for us. Make us sensitive to the persons we meet or are associated with today. Grant that our lives will be at your disposal. As we meet people, we pray that our words and actions will express something of your Spirit.

O Lord, open our eyes to some beauty of this day—in the world of nature about us, in the people around us, and in the conditions of which we are a part.

Make us good stewards of the fleeting hours of this day. In our work, make us faithful. In our play, make us free. In our associations, make us genuine. In our trials, make us strong. May all be enriched by your grace, through Christ our Lord. Amen.

28

STORMS OF LIFE

Then out of the storm the Lord spoke to Job.
Job 38:1 (TEV)

O Lord our God, in the midst of the storms of our lives, we pray that we may hear your Word. Gracious God, we believe that you have a word for us in every storm and time of need:

In the storms unique to childhood or youth, to middle years or aging,
In the storm of emotions,
In the storm of hasty words,
In the storm of conflicting relationships,
In the storm of disappointments and heartaches,
In the storm of sorrow and loss,
In the storm of fear and loneliness,
In the storm of illness,
In the storm of evil that beats upon us,
In the storm of death.

O Master, as you spoke on behalf of the disciples to the storm on the Sea of Galilee, "Peace be still, and there was a great calm," speak your Word of steadfast love, forgiveness, and peace to every troubled heart.

Speak to us, O blessed Lord, the Word we so much need to hear in this time of our need.

We pray for listening hearts to receive your Word of wisdom and calm.

Grant us the attitude of Samuel, who long ago said in the temple, "Speak, Lord, for thy servant heareth." May all those who join us now in that same prayer be especially blessed as they hear your Word to them. In your holy name we ask this. Amen.

On the day I called, thou didst answer me,
my strength of soul thou didst increase.
Psalm 138:3

Holy Father, thank you for listening to our call upon you. You are always there:

Listening to the cries of our hearts.

Listening to even the faintest whisper of our voices.

Listening to our unspoken prayers.

Listening to the throbbing of our desires.

Listening to and feeling with compassion the pain of our suffering in mind, body, and spirit.

Listening to our loneliness when we feel that no one cares what happens to us.

Listening to our prayers, O Lord, for the forgiveness of our sins and the salvation of our souls.

Listening to our prayers of intercessions for loved ones, friends, and others.

Listening to our prayers for healing and guidance.

We praise your holy name, O Lord, for answered prayers. Teach us that you know what is best for us in any given situation. Grant us the wisdom to receive your answers to our prayers in the same spirit in which the answers come.

We give thanks, Almighty God, for the strength of soul you have granted us. With the passing of the days, may our strength of soul continue to be increased by your grace. Help us to stand against temptations and for what is right in the power of your Holy Spirit. Amen.

Therefore we do not lose heart.
Though outwardly we are wasting away,
yet inwardly we are being renewed day by day.
For our light and momentary troubles
are achieving for us an eternal glory
that far outweighs them all.
So we fix our eyes not on what is seen,
but on what is unseen.
For what is seen is temporal,
but what is unseen is eternal.
2 Corinthians 4:16–18 (NIV)

Our Father God, we praise your name for your accepting and empowering grace that keeps us from losing heart even in adverse circumstances.

We thank you, Lord, for the strength of mind, body and spirit that comes from you day by day. We are renewed daily by your Holy Spirit. Because our bodies are earthen vessels of clay they will perish, but inwardly we draw upon the resources of heaven. We taste the powers of the world to come and are filled with hope.

O Lord, we thank you that the afflictions, sufferings and troubles of this life cannot be compared with the eternal glory in your kingdom.

Almighty God, we pray for your forgiveness for our sins of focusing our lives upon the things that perish. Help us to realize that life does not consist in the things we possess, but in our being possessed by our Master, Jesus Christ.

O Christ, you who are the light of the world, may your light shine with increasing brightness in our hearts so that the "things of earth will grow strangely dim" and the things of the Spirit will be magnified as we seek first your kingdom and your righteousness. We offer our prayer in your holy name. Amen.

29

OBEDIENCE
TO THE WORD

But he said, "Blessed rather are those who hear
the Word of God and obey it!"
Luke 11:28 (NRSV)

O Lord, we thank you not only for physical ears to hear the sound of your Word as it is read and spoken, but also for hearts to hear your Word in the depths of our being. We pray that our hearts will be open and receptive to your Word for us today. Help us to listen to your voice in our hearts before we go forth to hear the sounds of the world about us.

God of grace and God of glory, we pray for grace to be obedient to your Word as you speak to us in the now. We confess our sins of failing to listen for your Word and failing to obey your Word. We pray for your mercy and forgiveness.

Dear Master, may we be so faithful to you that we can echo the words of St. Paul when he stood before King Agrippa and said, "I was not disobedient to the heavenly vision" (Acts 26:19). May we not wait for some distant vision, but be obedient in living out your Word and will in the now.

In our times of testing and trials, grant that we will be undergirded by the witness and power of your Holy Spirit.

Increase our faith and deepen our obedience that your will, not ours, will be done in and through us. O Lord, cut your Word so deeply into our hearts that we will not sin against you, but we will show our joy in the promises of your Word by our obedience. Use us today in some way to be a blessing to others in the name of Christ our Lord. Amen.

If any one asks you, "Why are you untying it?"
You shall say this, "The Lord has need of it."
Luke 19:31

Dear Master, as we reflect on your riding into Jerusalem on the colt that was freely untied for you, we pray that our lives will be freely untied from self and released in your service.

O Lord, enable us by your grace to let go of whatever hinders us from being obedient to your call and command.

Grant that we will see clearly what you need of us:

You need our minds to think your thoughts.

You need our wills to be completely surrendered to your will.

You need our time when we are still and wait in prayer.

You need our weaknesses to show us how strong we may become in your divine power.

You need our illnesses that you may reveal to us your healing touch.

You need our material gifts that your church may advance the gospel of Christ throughout the world.

You need our worship that you may speak your Word to us and that we may glorify you.

In short, you need the work we can do and the witness we can give in your name. Forgive us from withholding anything that you would use. Truly all that we have is a gift from you. Grant us the grace to give as you have so freely given to us in your steadfast love. Amen.

He has showed you, O man, what is good;
and what does the Lord require of you but to do justice,
and to love kindness, and to walk humbly with your God.
Micah 6:8

O Lord God our Creator, we give praise to you for our creation. You have called us into being. It is also to you that we will return to give an account of our deeds in the body.

Gracious God, we thank you for the revelation of yourself through the people of Israel and in the fullness of time in Jesus Christ.

We confess our injustices done to other persons and our failure to be merciful. In our pride, we have walked in our own way, away from you.

Merciful God, we pray for a spirit of true repentance for our sins and we pray for your pardoning mercy. So transform our hearts that we may walk with you in abiding communion. May your presence be even more real to us than breath itself.

Gracious father, open our eyes today that we may see the needs of other persons and by your grace, help meet those needs. Make all of our human relationships reflect something of your love. May your Holy Spirit give us wisdom to guide us in the complexities of human relationships. Use us always as the Spirit of the Lord takes control of us in the furtherance of the gospel of Christ.

Lord God, as we pray with your Word sharpening our thoughts, grant that the Word will become enfleshed in us and will shine through us by the Spirit of Christ. Amen.

Do not lay up for yourselves treasures on earth,
where moth and rust consume
and where thieves break in and steal,
but lay up for yourselves treasures in heaven,
where neither moth nor rust consumes
and where thieves do not break in and steal.
For where your treasure is,
there will your heart be also.
Matthew 6:19–21

O Lord, you know the struggles that go on in our hearts to be good stewards of our material blessings and our spiritual lives. Help us to see that material things are useful in their place, but that life in the Spirit has the priority. We pray that the temporal things will be viewed as means, and never as ends in themselves.

We thank you, Lord, for the daily provisions of body and soul. We pray for those who hunger and thirst for sustenance of body, that they may be satisfied and be well. Grant your grace to all who hunger and thirst in heart, that their yearnings of soul will be answered with the abundance of your grace. We pray that all of us will be one with the Christ who said, "My food is to do the will of him who sent me" (John 4:34). Cleanse our hearts of sinful pride and grant that our lives will be centered in doing your will.

Gracious God, we pray that we will know the reality of your presence in the simple things of daily living. Help us to pray with Ingatius Loyola, "to labor and not ask for any reward save that of knowing that we do thy will." Amen.

I keep the Lord always before me;
because he is at my right hand, I shall not be moved.
Psalm 16:8

Heavenly Father, as we face each new day, help us to keep you before us whether we are going out into the wider world of business or travel, or are at home, or are in the hospital. Go before us, O Lord, with your prevenient grace and prepare our minds and hearts to face what lies ahead of us with confidence in your love and wisdom.

O Lord, we believe that when you are at our right hand we will not be moved to make some detour from the path of your will. We praise your name, gracious God, when your hand has rested firmly upon us at critical moments of temptation and made us strong in your grace for victory in Christ Jesus.

O God, without your help we are not able to please you, so grant us the presence and power of your Holy Spirit, who enables us to do your will. Transform our weaknesses into strengths. Overcome our fears with the wonder of trusting in you.

As Jesus steadfastly set his face to go to Jerusalem, knowing that crucifixion awaited him, O Lord, we pray for steadfastness of mind and heart to be obedient to your will, whatever the cost.

God of power and might, we pray that your promise, "Thou dost keep him in perfect peace, whose mind is stayed on thee" (Isa. 26:3), will be fulfilled in our lives. May our minds be locked in on obedience to your will and way, and may our hearts be filled with your peace in the name of the Prince of Peace. Amen.

Do not remove the ancient landmark
that your ancestors set up.
Proverbs 22:28 (NRSV)

Gracious God, we thank you for the landmarks that our ancestors have set up, by your grace and wisdom, to guide us on the highway of life. Empower us by your Holy Spirit to follow these landmarks.

May the landmark of the Commandments be kept before us. We pray for grace and wisdom to love you with our whole beings, to love our neighbors as ourselves, and to keep your commandments.

May we trust the landmarks of your promises, "In all your ways acknowledge him, and he will make straight your paths" (Prov. 3:6).

Lord, may we always remember to trust and follow the landmark you set up for Moses and us, "I will be with you" (Exod. 3:12).

Eternal God, we pray that in the rush of life, our vision will not be blurred. Help us to pause gratefully before the landmark, "They who wait for the Lord shall renew their strength. They shall run and not be weary, they shall walk and not faint" (Isa. 40:31).

May the landmark, "In everything God works for good with those who love him, who are called according to his purpose," (Rom. 8:28) guide us through dark nights, tragedy, sorrow, and uncertainty.

Above all, O Lord, grant that the landmark that guided Jesus' life, "My food is to do the will of him who sent me" (Mark 4:34), may be our daily guide. Help us to see that it is in losing life, in surrendering life to Christ, and in letting him be our Master, that we find life with ultimate meaning and purpose. We pray for our lives to be so transformed by your grace that they might point others in the path of true life in Christ's name. Amen.

ABOUT THE AUTHOR

W. Aubrey Alsobrook served as pastor for forty years in the South Georgia and New Jersey Annual Conferences of the United Methodist Church, serving both rural and urban churches. He received his bachelor's degrees in philosophy and divinity from Emory University and his doctoral degree from Drew University.

An active writer, for twenty-five years he has authored an interpretation of the International Series Sunday School Lessons for the fall quarter in the *Wesleyan Christian Advocate*. His writings have also appeared in other church publications. He is a frequent columnist for the *Americus-Times Recorder*.